Playing

Playing for Real

Actors on Playing Real People

Edited by

Tom Cantrell and Mary Luckhurst

To John,
for inspiring my
love of theatre.
Many, many thanks

palgrave
macmillan

First published 2010 by
PALGRAVE MACMILLAN

Palgrave Macmillan in the UK is an imprint of Macmillan Publishers Limited, registered in England, company number 785998, of Houndmills, Basingstoke, Hampshire RG21 6XS.

Palgrave Macmillan in the US is a division of St Martin's Press LLC, 175 Fifth Avenue, New York, NY 10010.

Palgrave Macmillan is the global academic imprint of the above companies and has companies and representatives throughout the world.

Palgrave® and Macmillan® are registered trademarks in the United States, the United Kingdom, Europe and other countries.

ISBN-13: 978–0–230–23041–5 hardback
ISBN-13: 978–0–230–23042–2 paperback

This book is printed on paper suitable for recycling and made from fully managed and sustained forest sources. Logging, pulping and manufacturing processes are expected to conform to the environmental regulations of the country of origin.

A catalogue record for this book is available from the British Library.

A catalog record for this book is available from the Library of Congress.

10   9   8   7   6   5   4   3   2   1
19 18 17 16 15 14 13 12 11 10

Printed in China

for Chris Kay
who claims he is the only real man I have ever met
– Mary

and for Peter Raby and Steve Waters
for inspiration and encouragement
– Tom

Contents

Acknowledgements

This book was funded, in part, by the Higher Education Academy, sponsors of a three-year drama project led by Mary Luckhurst. We are indebted to them. The editors are very grateful to the actors who gave up their time to talk to us. All of them had full schedules but focused on the project with passion and energy, and without them there would be no book. We would like to thank the actors for giving permission to print their interviews. The idea for this volume was dreamt up on a train journey to Steve Waters's 'From Fact to Fiction' conference at the University of Birmingham, a tribute to just how inspiring Steve can be – even at a distance.

Our warmest appreciation goes to Kate Haines at Palgrave who was the best combination of excitement and commitment; and to Penny Simmons for her care and enthusiasm. We would also like to thank Christy Adair, Richard Coyle, Fraser Grace, Ronald Harwood, Max Stafford-Clark and Charles Wood for their help. Deepest thanks also to Andy Tudor and Mike Cordner who were, as always, tremendously supportive and never less than brilliant (though they rarely stopped reminiscing about Cyd Charisse's legs). Our appreciation also goes to Andrea Potts and all in the Department of Theatre, Film and Television at the University of York, the most creative and inspiring of work places. Simon Callow and Siân Phillips were both very pro-active and kind. Derek Paget and his team of documentary researchers at the University of Reading have provided much intellectual encouragement. Mary road-tested the introduction in Australia. Staff and students at NIDA, the University of New South Wales and Latrobe University proved very stimulating audiences – special thanks to Peter Eckersall, Meg Mumford, Karen Vickery, Anthony Skuse and Peta Tait. During her time in Australia, Mary was buoyed by the fantastic warmth (not to mention food and wine) of Chris Kay and his friends: thanks to Drew 'Poke it!' Davy and Katrina G; Chris and Margaret; Jeff 'have you seen the size of my scar?' Maher and Tara; Vikki and Donald; and last but not least, Murray and Marie and their Whispering Hills winery. (Apologies to Cate B. – blame the man in

Melbourne.) Chris Hogg, Ollie Jones, Doug 'Brando' Kern and Nik Morris are legends in the making. Victoria Coulson was a stunning intellectual asset and provided high-quality chocolate. Kate Lovell and Michael Lightfoot offered regular theatrical fixes. Thanks to Alastair Ross for Leeds, Chelsea and trips to the capital; and to Richard, Rosie and Rachel Cantrell for their pearls of wisdom, and finally to Robert Waiting of the Cambridge Explorers, for all-round brilliance.

Introduction: Research, Acting Strategies, and Performer and Audience

Mary Luckhurst

For the last two decades theatre, film and television have reflected a growing obsession with the real throughout the world. Public appetite for representations of the real and for exhaustive information on real people is evident not just on television and radio, but also in newspapers and magazines, on the web, in the fashion for blockbuster biographies and all the paraphernalia of celebrity culture mechanisms, including the emergent academic discipline of celebrity studies. Despite the explosion of interest in representing persons of historical and contemporary significance on stage and on screen, there has been virtually no attempt to examine this phenomenon from an actor's perspective. This book aims to open up a new area for theatre research.

Established actors and newcomers report that they are increasingly offered parts based on persons of note. 'How many real people can one man play?', asked Michael Pennington in an article for the *Guardian* in 2008, in which he gave an account of how he was about to play his tenth historical figure in a row.[1] Dramatists and screenwriters such as Charles Wood have also observed that producers are now far more likely to encourage writers to submit scripts about real people than invented characters.[2] Without doubt, the critical academies currently confer greater prestige on actors who perform roles based on an actual person. In this respect the Oscar awards for Best Actor and Best Actress over the last 15 years make for instructive reading. The list includes: Geoffrey Rush as David Helfgott in *Shine* (1996); Julia Roberts as the eponymous heroine Erin Brockovich (2000); Nicole Kidman as Virginia Woolf in *The Hours* (2002); Charlize Theron as

Aileen Wuornos in *Monster* (2003); Jamie Foxx as Ray Charles in *Ray* (2004); Forest Whittaker as Idi Amin in *Last King of Scotland* (2006); Helen Mirren as Queen Elizabeth II in *The Queen* (2006); and Sean Penn as Harvey Milk in *Milk* (2008). In Britain, one of the most famous recipients of two BAFTA awards, Judi Dench, won them for playing Queen Victoria in *Mrs Brown* (1997) and the writer Iris Murdoch in *Iris* (2001). Michael Sheen, one of the most celebrated actors of the moment, has won his international reputation, as well as an OBE (in 2009), for his portrayals of real people – including Kenneth Williams, Tony Blair, David Frost and Brian Clough.[3]

Is it possible to identify differences between preparing for and acting a real person and preparing for and acting a fictional character? What are the specific challenges of playing a real person as opposed to a fictional one? Is there a greater sense of anxiety or of responsibility when representing a person of repute? How do individual actors prepare for such parts? Are the risks to one's career greater when playing a real person? How important is it to the success of a project that the actor can evoke a physical resemblance to their subject? Are actors cast on the basis of their looks? How do actors go about conjuring particular kinds of greatness, celebrity or genius? How do actors measure audience expectations against their own interpretation of a well-known figure? Does playing a real person involve a different set of techniques or preoccupations for the actor? Does playing in a documentary drama involve challenges which are specific to the genre?[4] This book of interviews makes a first step towards considering some of these questions. All of the actors interviewed approach their roles in different ways, but all are of the view that the subject of playing real people has been a neglected territory. Acting is a notoriously tricky process to analyse, and all actors noted the difficulty of finding a language to describe their thoughts and feelings about playing someone who has actually lived or is still living.

My co-editor and I do not regard this volume as a workbook or manual on how to act real people – it would be presumptuous to draw hard and fast conclusions on the basis of 16 interviews. The actors interviewed were speaking only for themselves and none advocated a fixed approach. We did not ask each actor the same set of questions because our pre-preparation indicated that many would find this inhibiting and inappropriate. We let actors choose what they wished to reflect on and did not ask 'leading' questions which contained the names of acting practitioners. Oliver Ford Davies preferred to write out his response because he wanted to formulate his thoughts in his own time. We did approach more female actors than appear in this volume but the fullness of their work schedules thwarted us. All actors edited and amended transcripts as they saw fit: the interview itself was treated as a first step towards articulating processes, which the 16 actors had thought about a good deal but rarely, if ever, discussed with others.

We have simply let the interviews stand because we would have needed to conduct many more interviews to begin to make informed theoretical assertions.[5] None the less, the volume contains many fascinating and useful insights for trainee and established actors, and for students and devotees of drama. The interviews have thrown up more matters for perusal than I could easily accommodate in an introduction, so I have selected three major areas which I think provide useful frames for consideration: researching the part; acting strategies; and performer and audience. It is certainly possible, even at this early stage, to identify some common and quite intriguing preoccupations.

Researching the part

Most actors argued that research facilitated their performances, but also stressed the importance of acquiring an ability to select and distil information which serves the construction of the person created for the specific production. David Morrissey read biographies and Gordon Brown's own books, voraciously watched footage, met people who knew Brown privately and publicly, and visited the town where Brown had grown up.

> I always find it very important to work out exactly where your character comes from, especially if they are real people. Who are his parents? What did they do? Who were his grandparents? Where did he grow up and what was happening in his formative years? [...] A lot of the research you can't use because it might not be relevant to the script but I find very significant insights working this way. [...] When you play a real person you don't take anything for granted – if information or an environment is there and it's tangible, I try to seek it out. There are things you can only learn for yourself.

Similarly, Elena Roger immersed herself in the places that Edith Piaf had frequented in Paris and came to understand the dictates of poverty in the singer's life. Oliver Ford Davies absorbed the urban landscapes of Hull in his attempts to fathom Philip Larkin. Henry Goodman finds research essential to his creative process, and a means of establishing his own intellectual and emotional response to the subject he is performing. 'Research', he asserts, 'liberates the creative instincts' and allows the actor to understand his received impressions of the person he is playing:

> Once you start rehearsing a play, it seems to me that even if you don't have that overt, articulate debate with yourself (which I enjoy but which a lot of actors don't), you are forced through the process of rehearsal and discussion to notice the assumptions that you make and either affirm or challenge them. [...] You can't create a performance by reading books about things, but you can get assurance, comfort and support as well as new ideas for instincts that may come to you from the script. Even when you're playing a real person the writer may have invented a view of this person: that view might be bold and against the public perceptions that you have absorbed. In reading around you can determine for yourself what constructions the author is conforming to or working against. You can fill in the gaps and glean information that can liberate your creative energy.

Goodman echoes the warnings of many of the actors in this book who argue that it is 'a fatal mistake to try and act your research.' Actors must ultimately focus on the part as it appears in the script and Michael Pennington issues a stark warning that if an actor cannot distil useful points of research and discard the unhelpful information, 'you can hang by your own shoelaces'. It is all too easy, he asserts, 'to become obsessed by historical reality and lose your connection with the fictional world of the drama'. In a radio interview Michael Sheen has contended that a greater amount of research is needed if the actor is playing a living or recently deceased person: 'The audience is going to be very familiar with them, so you do have to meet the audience's demand for familiarity.'[6] Morrissey certainly supports this view, but also argues that the more influential a living subject is, the greater the responsibility to represent the situations in which they are depicted with accuracy. Research is never complete when performing a living and powerful politician in dramas such as *The Deal*, Morrissey asserts, and the actor, director and production team must be constantly alert to the ever-changing political situation:

> If information comes in repeatedly which contradicts what's in the script you *have* to deal with it. You must keep an eye on the information flow as an actor playing a real person. Like a journalist, you have to be able to corroborate your decision with facts, not hearsay. You can't play fast and loose with the public.

Reading is only one aspect of the actor's possible research tasks. Not all actors do background reading, and this can be a matter of preference or force of necessity. In fact, the absence of narrative and the material conditions of production may not permit research. There is, for example, no time for discussion on a shooting set. McKellen draws attention to the fact that Shakespeare's representation of monarchs such as Richard III is decidedly creative; Phillips recalls that scarcely anything was known about Livia in Ancient Rome for *I, Claudius*, but makes the important point that costumiers and make-up artists were expected to do rigorous research of their own; and Roger Allam found the lack of preparation time when he was cast to play Hitler a liberating experience. 'One can read too much and play the research rather than the role.' His preparation time was rushed and abrupt because of production and personal circumstances, but as a result he felt that he was 'more open to suggestion' and was more content 'to just dive in and try things out.'

On the other hand, performers are usually greatly helped by visual and audio recordings, and Diane Fletcher speaks for many when she emphasises that the actor's powers of observation and listening, and their facility for noticing behavioural detail are the most important aspects of their research method. Ian McKellen and Simon Callow draw attention to this, too, and Elena Roger argues that observation is fundamental to the actor's preparation: 'The real job of the actor is about observation: to observe all the time, everything and everybody.'[7] One of the ironies of playing someone of note, however, is the excessive amount of material that might be in the public domain. Callow points out that the actor can be overwhelmed by a surfeit of information, and both he and Eileen Atkins have found themselves in a position where their own research has provoked more interest in them than has the script they have been reading. Goodman, Callow and Atkins refer diplomatically to disagreements they have had with writers and directors about the interpretation of the figure they have been playing.

As Ford Davies points out, actors are more often required to portray the private selves of public figures and therefore tend to find diaries, letters, memoirs and home videos particularly revealing. The reliability of secondary material about persons of repute is a difficult issue for some actors. Atkins and Roger, in particular, are sceptical about biographies and historical accounts, indeed Atkins regards the inventions and fancies of biographers and historians of figures such as Elizabeth I and Virginia Woolf as greatly adding to the 'big problem about playing real people is you read all this stuff [...] but people make things up to make their little idea work, to make it all fit in.' There is no such thing as the truth, argues Atkins, and similarly Roger came to distrust the agendas behind many of the accounts she read about the Argentinean legend Eva Peron. Nevertheless, both actresses informed themselves of the many differing perspectives on their subjects, and selected useful nuggets of information for themselves. Atkins also highlights issues about received impressions of celebrities and the mass circulation of certain images which show only a brief, posed moment in time, but are often treated as though they reveal something profound and authentic about the person. Similarly, though talking to relatives, friends, lovers or colleagues can be helpful in finding out about a subject, memory can function in a curious and very unreliable way – as Jeremy Irons, McKellen and Atkins attest.

Acting strategies

A major consideration for actors performing real people is the tactical issue of how far they seek to resemble their subject physically. The question, as Callow, poses it, is 'to what extent you can ever play a person that lived?', and he argues that 'you can certainly capture their external mannerisms' – providing you have the information. The decision about the degree of external detail an actor might pursue is both a matter of personal preference and of forecasting the audience's expectations of what might constitute a convincing portrayal of a specific individual. The more historically remote the person, the lower the risk of alienating spectators, Pennington claims. Goodman is of the same view and contends that the currency of the person being played affects the actor's approach to the part and the audience's reception of it: the more images and vocal imprints that have been circulated close to the time of production, the greater the necessity to pay close attention to external details. Phillips is rather more blunt in her formulation:

> There is a general thing about playing real people which is that when they are dead, you are off the hook (to a certain extent). When you are playing real people who have died recently, or who are still alive, it is a nightmare. It is a ghastly responsibility for a start, because of families and descendents. There is obviously a limit to how far you can transform yourself into another person, with the best will in the world.

All actors agreed that film and television demand a greater specificity than theatre where appearance is concerned because of the mediation of the camera and the viewer's magnified proximity to the actor's face and body on screen. Pennington posits that the camera is more unforgiving:

> I suspect that more people come out of a film prepared to be openly critical if someone doesn't look like the person he or she is playing. I think for theatre audiences there is a greater sense of playfulness and a tolerance of what you might be up to as an actor. Theatre audiences are quite quick to note the decisions you have made in respect to playing the role and they travel with you.

Pennington's suggestion is that theatre audiences are more willing to suspend disbelief than film spectators and this was a commonly held opinion among the actors we interviewed. Advances in costuming and make-up, and inventions such as the body suit, have made the business of resemblance a much more sophisticated and exact art than it used to be, but the fact that acting time is not continuous in film makes it much easier for actors to reach for such elaborate detail on screen. Morrissey, for example, is scrupulous in acknowledging the assistance of costumiers, hairdressers and make-up artists in the

...ı of Gordon Brown. But the significance of an
...ed to be convincing to themselves and to find a
...ı their subject is not to be downplayed in theatre
...nt actors take recourse to different strategies accord-
...ıey are performing. For Ford Davies finding the looks
of ı... ...is essential:

> It's hard to overestimate how important it is to feel you look like
> the subject. It not only boosts your confidence, it persuades you
> or, more probably, kids you that something of him is coursing
> through you. As you first step before the audience you need to
> feel that they will accept you as a plausible representation of the
> person in question.

Roger Allam echoes this in his comments on playing Hitler, and
describes how 'extremely important' it was to find a satisfactory
likeness because 'he comes with a set of iconic visual characteristics and physical mannerisms' and 'you have to be convincing to
the audience.' Allam did not feel the same intensity of pressure to
resemble either politician Willy Brandt or the theatre impresario Max
Reinhardt because both were far less notorious and their images much
less circulated. For Allam, altering his hair and eyebrows and growing a moustache proved to be the key factors in recreating Hitler's
look. Atkins invests in the magical art of make-up rather than devices
such as false noses – 'people were utterly astonished at the make up
for Elizabeth I.'[8] Atkins speaks of the importance of wigs. Phillips
explains the almost fetishistic way in which she re-created the image
of Marlene Dietrich, including using the same wigmaker, the original lighting plot, and a dressmaker who copied the star's costume
'down to the number of glass pendants'. Joseph Mydell talks of the
breakthrough of finding Robert Mugabe's physicality through a certain way of holding his shoulders and jutting his head forward,
and of discovering the dictator's deadly authority by thinking of his
body as a military tank. Goodman and Irons stress the psychological detective work in figuring out how to play a real person, and
Goodman recalls that Roy Cohn's passing reference to wearing an
orange jacket was a vital clue to this lawyer's vanity and flamboyance.
In preparing to play Elizabeth II, Helen Mirren turned to voice and
physicality:

The voice was terribly important. The voice and the physicality. [...] I studied a great deal of film just to watch her: the way she walks, the way she holds her head, what she does with her hands, exactly where the handbag is held, when she wears her glasses and when she doesn't wear her glasses, which is quite interesting. When there's a tension and when there's a relaxation.[9]

Pennington and Callow, on the other hand, are fascinated by the physical and psychological effect of a man's profession on his body, and Michael Chekhov's practice of identifying a 'psychological gesture', a stance or gesture which supposedly captures a fundamental quality about a person, is a useful tool for Callow. Learning to engrave like Raimondi had done, Callow realised that the engraver's hands would always have been covered in ink; learning *Le Nozze de Figaro* off by heart, Callow came to understand something of Mozart's obsessional internal world. West, on the other hand, warns against excessive attention to physical attributes, reliving the nightmare of playing Winston Churchill with false ears, a false nose, a hair-piece, and contact lenses which gave him tunnel vision. When he played the part again, he found a greater credibility in the voice, cigar, spotted bow-tie and 'various hats.' What mattered to West was the 'psychological vignette', though he is clear that the actor still has 'to find a distillation of that public figure, to reduce and naturalise it. You have to convince the audience that you've done your homework, visually and vocally.'

Most actors emphasise the importance of finding a credible voice or accent, McKellen insisting that the voice is 'easier to capture' than the face, which is 'impossible' to capture in its volatility. Morrissey highlights the vital support of voice coaches. Finding a convincing voice is clearly essential for playing real people who were or are singers, performers and orators, and Elena Roger's version of Piaf and Siân Phillips's incarnation of Marlene Dietrich have become celebrated in their own right. Allam and West speak of the challenge of finding an accented English for a non-English-speaking subject, and West recounts his process for inventing his version of Joseph Stalin's Georgian accent. Irons found that Harold Macmillan's habit of concealing his blackened teeth by lowering his top lip accounted for the way he spoke. Atkins and Phillips reveal their tussle to find a workable voice for Virginia Woolf, and Phillips explains how she found the rhythms of Woolf's voice and writing useful, but rejected her RP accent because she feared that contemporary audiences would think it 'affected'. Phillips discusses the difficulty of balancing the reality of the sound of a voice with commonly believed myths about it, which in turn shape audience expectation. When she played the nineteenth-century actress Mrs Patrick Campbell, Phillips discovered that popular history had rewritten Campbell's 'light and very quick voice' as 'booming' and 'actressy'. As a result, she felt she had to 'steer a middle course' to satisfy audiences – even though received wisdom was 'completely wrong'. Phillips also famously played Marlene Dietrich and ultimately found that getting the voice right was the key to unlocking her performance, that the songs were the means by which she could understand her. 'Copying' Dietrich's cabaret performance, Phillips worked with a musical director for months, reproducing exact phrasing, accent and breathing patterns.

Siân Phillips's account of performing Dietrich is particularly fascinating because, in this collection of interviews, it is one of the few in which an actor discusses the painstaking art of imitation. For the last 30 minutes of Pam Gems's play *Marlene*, Phillips re-enacted Dietrich's cabaret routine and sang some of her most legendary songs. Phillips describes the laborious process of copying 'every finger movement, every gesture on every note she sang', and of taking weeks to absorb material so that she could copy Dietrich's postures and style of walking as accurately as possible. Despite what she calls the 'agony' of the 'surface' work, her technical mastery of Dietrich's physicality and voice enabled her to get into the part. The analogy she uses for this kind of concentrated focus on external detail is her experience of once being directed by Samuel Beckett in *Eh Joe*:

That was a challenge because he [Beckett] taps his finger like a metronome and you have to count the full stops, commas, semi-colons, they all counted. So preparing a text with him is a purely mechanical and tortured affair. You have no contribution of your own at all. You are a machine trying to do it. Lots of actors won't do it, but I got it into my head that I would stick it out and see where it went. In the end, I realised it was the only way to do the play. It became second nature – I couldn't imagine doing it any other way. The mechanical work suddenly became real, became personal, it was strange. But the point is, the same happened with

Marlene, the external, the minute details one worked on didn't feel at all useful and then suddenly it all came together and one feels like someone else.

Phillips's description is reminiscent of the dancer or athlete learning physical technique which finally liberates them into a full and strong performance. As she recounts the process, psychological access to the character is gained through mastery of the physical, and not vice versa and this initially felt alien to Phillips. Diane Fletcher echoes Phillips's comments about the punishing nature of imitation in her reflections on playing the politician Clare Short, using interview footage of her as her source material. The play was a verbatim project so Fletcher was also speaking Short's own words.

I suppose I did my normal process backwards. I have always thought of myself as an actor who works out how the thought affects physicality, but here I had to do it the other way round: I had to work out what she was thinking from the way she was moving, which fascinated me. [...] I couldn't allow myself interpretation, which is usually the critical role of the actor. I actually found it very tiring. Exhausting.

Fletcher elaborates on how she could not always match thought to action in her reconstruction of Short's performance, and at such moments simply copied the movement. Unlike Phillips, who went on to give numerous performances of *Marlene*, Fletcher felt that her stamina was at full stretch and was grateful that the run was limited.

Imitation as an art has received very little analytical attention, and Phillips is a rare actor in her usage of the word in relation to herself. Both Phillips and Fletcher recount a requirement in the play for documentary precision, but in this book of interviews actors are mostly discussing parts which were the invention not of the subjects in question, but of the writers. Michael Sheen, like many actors, does not feel it describes what he does when he plays real people:

Impersonation tends to be satirical or involve a sketch. What I do has to involve a whole journey, a whole narrative. I have to find a balance and incorporate enough of the external stuff – voice, mannerisms and physicality – to satisfy an audience.[10]

The majority of actors in this volume renounce imitation as a description of what they do, but frequently use Sheen and the stand-up comedian, Rory Bremner, as points of reference to highlight sets of skills they feel are different from their own. McKellen enjoys physical routes into a role and professes to be 'fascinated by impersonators', but is clear that he uses external details as clues to how that person's psychological profile might be affected: he does not 'copy' externals, but works out how they affect 'internal mechanisms.' His interpretation of Hitler, for example, was informed by his realisation that there was damage to his back which affected the way he held himself. West selects and copies certain external features and also uses them as psychological data: he talks eloquently about the paralysis in Stalin's left arm and its emotional effect on him. Impersonation, for the actors in this book, is understood as an ability to mimic the physical qualities of a person and is not associated with complex emotional journeys. But this is a raw definition of an art that most actors in this volume feel they neither understand nor master, and their views on impersonation often betray an assumption that a facility to reproduce the external qualities of a person is a less noble art than the ability to create a figure who journeys through emotional depths. As McKellen phrases it: 'Impersonation is entertaining [...] acting is not just about appearances, it is about the inner life.' The two skills cannot, in fact, be mutually exclusive and have long been unhelpfully polarised. To add to the confusion McKellen also observes that 'all acting is impersonation in a sense.'

As West points out, actors are often invoking the private selves of a real person, not just the public personae (though the documentary form often tends to concentrate on the public). Private moments allow actors to be inventive, and indeed Phillips says that she was far less anxious about playing Dietrich off the stage in Act I of *Marlene* because so much less was known about her. But the performance of a real person's private faces is also a distinct challenge – how, for example, wondered West when he was performing Winston Churchill, did this great public rhetorician ask his wife for a cup of tea? Iron's understood Macmillan's repressed homosexuality as a vital feature of his character, but how do you perform what was not acknowledged – even to himself? Similarly, how did Stalin behave with close friends? How do you make decisions about Queen Elizabeth II's or Tsar Nicholas's behaviour behind closed doors? Most actors are looking for the acting note which goes beyond the media stereotype or received idea of their subject: Atkins, for instance, became intrigued by Virginia Woolf's humour and waspish tongue and came to feel that she had been too often represented as monolithically depressed. Mydell saw that the death of Mugabe's son had made him desperately vulnerable, and that he wasn't just 'a monster'. For *The Queen*, Helen Mirren found her private tea with Elizabeth II an invaluable insight into her humour and private informality.[11]

An actor's celebrity status can also have an effect on his or her approach to playing a real person, and the degree to which they might find disguise appealing. Rojek has discussed what he terms 'the spillover effect between the role incarnated by the actor in performance and the public perception of the actor.'[12] Irons acknowledged that audiences probably came more to see him perform Macmillan than for the playwright's representation of Macmillan. Irons debated with himself whether to reproduce Macmillan's famously rotten teeth, but ironised his own celebrity with the observation that: 'One thing I discovered was that Jeremy Irons doesn't do bad teeth!' Irons, then, makes it clear that he did not want to lose the image of Irons on stage and set limits to the process of transformation. McKellen is intriguing about the dominance of McKellen the actor over the real people he has played. He is sceptical about the whole subject of resemblance and thinks it very difficult if not impossible to achieve. Of the British film director James Whale, McKellen argues:

> I did talk to people who knew Whale, and interestingly they all told me something different. They talked about the Whale they knew. You see, we exist in the minds of other people, so our outward appearances are not the sum of who we are. To the people who really knew James Whale I didn't look like him. I looked like Ian McKellen playing James Whale. That is what I am when I am playing anything.

For Irons and McKellen, the greater the celebrity status the less need there may be to resemble the person in question, because audience expectations may be focused more on the actor than the role. Other high-profile actors are fascinated by the art of transformation. Olivier is perhaps the most famous example, but Callow is also a believer, not in transformation as disguise, 'but in the revelation of alternative possibilities in the muscular disposition of the face and body'.[13]

Performer and audience

Actors agree that playing a real person requires a different kind of preparation and thought process from performing a fictional character, although, as has already been made clear in this chapter, the nature of that preparation depends on the actor and the role. Ford Davies observes that:

> The parameters of playing a real person are different from fictional parameters. King Lear can be a tough old bull who should never have abdicated, or a frail man in the early stages of dementia – the text will support both readings. But with Napoleon you can't take such extreme positions – we [the actors] and the audience know too much about him. With a modern part, Margaret Thatcher, say, the choices are even more limited.

Actors feel a very particular sort of responsibility towards a real subject, which McKellen argues is a major difference from playing an invented figure: 'you want to do the right thing by them.' He echoes Phillips in pointing out that the risk of disapproval from the individual's family and friends is often significant. Morrissey worries about doing 'a disservice' to a man he personally respects. Pennington expresses his investment in terms of wanting to give a 'legitimate' performance, that is, one solidly rooted in research, careful reflection and observation. Mydell is highly conscious of the importance of being able to justify his interpretation of the dictator Mugabe: 'as an actor I had to be able to argue precisely, factually, intellectually what he had done prior to becoming this appalling man.' Phillips voices a common view when speaking of balancing out audience expectations with her own impression of a person. Whereas Allam talks of not letting 'his ego get in the way', Phillips says:

> With a real person you have to try and avoid letting too much of yourself seep in. [...] You can bend a fictional character to yourself much more, but you can't do that with real people.

This heightened sense of responsibility can weigh heavy: Morrissey describes a night wracked with anxiety and 'actor paranoia'; Fletcher talks of 'real terror'; and Sheen has spoken elsewhere of the recurring anxiety that no one will find his portrayals convincing.[14] Actors need to be able to justify their performative interpretation of a part both for themselves and for an audience. Two actors who were overwhelmed by this sense of responsibility were Chung and Fletcher, who both performed in verbatim plays. Both felt that documentary theatre, and specifically verbatim, in which the actual words of the person are spoken, required greater emotional restraint from the actor: 'the less outward theatricality you display, the more you serve the representation of the person you are playing.' Both felt that the emotional range an actor could play was narrower in documentary because it was not appropriate to indulge their own creativity as they do with a fictional person.

Of necessity, most representations of persons of note involve the portrayal of someone with exceptional ability or looks, or both, and often require the actor to suggest genius, charisma or star quality. Actors, therefore, are concerned with questions of how greatness might be suggested. Such qualities are in themselves extremely difficult to define, as Luckhurst and Moody, Roach, and Goodall have made clear.[15] Allam argues that representations of charisma can be fruitfully explored through the reactions of the other characters on stage. West, who, like Callow, believes that performing is 'essentially about thinking the thoughts of someone else', talks of the imaginative commitment to a part. If you are playing a dictator like Stalin or a serial killer like Bodkin Adams, he contends, you have to imagine that you have the power to end a life. Pennington voices one of the grittiest questions:

> How do you play a genius? Well, how do you recognise a genius across a coffee table? You don't. Probably a genius doesn't behave any more erratically or peculiarly than anyone else at first glance. But that's the question you have to engage with. How do you subliminally suggest that you are the person who could have written *Der Rosenkavalier* or *Great Expectations*?

Pennington does not have an answer but he speculates that provided the actor has researched and prepared carefully, it may also have something to do with the pact between performer and audience, and the energy, concentration and trust between them:

> It's a form of acting or a way of behaving where people are prepared to say yes, I believe he might have been something like this [...] The very fact of people being alert to what you are attempting to do is galvanizing. They positively want to believe it and in some mysterious way that makes it possible for you to do it.

Audiences do, of course, measure an actor's interpretation and own star quality against what they know of the person being represented – quantifying devices do exist when playing a real person in a way they do not for a fictional figure – and everyone can name a show where the actor has fallen on their face because they have failed in their ability to create a convincing portrayal.[16] On the whole, the actors we interviewed report positive experiences. What is striking about the material in this volume is that most actors have a sense of doubleness regarding their stage presence: generally, they both do and do not believe that they have achieved a likeness to their subject; they both do and do not believe that they have captured a 'distillation', or an 'essence' or a 'spirit'. Marlon Brando wrote that the actor's art is to manipulate human suggestibility,[17] and Irons was certainly conscious of the need to exercise a specific form of persuasion when playing Macmillan:

> In the first five minutes, you walk on and say: 'This is Macmillan. Forget what you know, or how I look because I don't look like him.'

Audience members, critics, and old colleagues and friends of Macmillan's, however, all told Irons that he looked exactly like him:

> People tell me I've captured Macmillan's gestures fantastically. Of course, I don't know his gestures, but I do know that gestures come from what you are feeling.

Goodman was intrigued by responses from spectators when he played Freud in Terry Johnson's *Hysteria*:

> The fascinating thing was that as soon as I opened my mouth and started playing, people thought: 'It's Freud! That's him – on

stage!' I was repeatedly told that I looked ju_
just like him, even though audience members
immediate memory. Many had never heard the ↙
voice nor seen footage of him and yet they though.
was amazing. It's a sort of social memory, an 'icon mem.

Most actors have an understandable (and sometimes terri._ _g)
sense of the gap between their subject and themselves, and are
delighted if a little bemused by the hyperbole that can attend their
portrayal. McKellen talks of the pressure to meet public expectations
when playing a real person, and argues that, for the audience, questions of intimacy are also at stake; part of his job, therefore, is 'to give
people that little bit of a thrill that they are getting close to an iconic
or famous person'. He muses on his own experience of watching Jane
Lapotaire playing Piaf and Prunella Scales playing Elizabeth II, thinking at moments in both productions that the singer and the monarch
were before him 'in the flesh'. Iconic people have 'certain characteristics to which we respond', McKellen contends, and the skilful
actor can identify and reproduce them. Given McKellen's celebrity
credentials, the factor of intimacy, no doubt, also pertains to himself.
In *The Presence of an Actor*, Chaikin makes some interesting reflections on expectation. Although he concentrates on the actor's point
of view, expectations are present in both performer and spectator and
can work powerfully together to create an effect of another's presence.

> Expecting a thing you are calling it up, you are making an open
> place for it to come in. You call on something in another which is
> also alive in yourself.[18]

Summoning the impression of a real person is, then, a collective
art, and relies on a curious concoction of belief and non-belief in
performer and spectator.

Chaikin also alludes to the doubleness an actor feels in performance, stating that 'the actor experiences a dialectic between
restraint and abandon; between impulse and the form that expresses
it; between the act and the way it is perceived by an audience.'[19] Iron-
ically, McKellen confesses to being most unnerved when he played
a version of himself for Ricky Gervais's *Extras*. Alienated by how he
chose to perform himself, McKellen has since altered his behaviour
for interviews: 'I try not to present myself too much.' Observing

...at humans are unknowable to themselves and act 'all day long', McKellen reminds us that the self is multivalent and fluid, and that actors of real people are often playing the most prevalently circulated received versions and images of that person, in other words – versions of mass versions.

It is a truism that actors must sympathise with their character if they are to play them well, but this is not always possible and the lack of identification an actor might feel for a part is a territory of strange taboo about which performers say little. Actors may find their relish for playing a real person precisely in their criminality, their brutality or ruthlessness – just as they do with celebrated dramatic villains. Antony Sher experienced a bizarre and joyous revenge playing Hitler in Brecht's *Arturo Ui*:

> Climbing into the skin of the enemy, feeling his power, all the thrill of that, yet positioned to poison him, weaken him, show him for what he is. I become him, you destroy him.[20]

Allam played Hitler 'sincerely', as a man who believed what he was doing. As Callow points out, dramatists often adhere to conventions about character which require their sanitisation, erasing contradiction and paradox for the sake of a coherent dramaturgy. What often interests actors the most about the challenge of playing a real person are the mysteries or stark contrasts about them. West speaks evocatively of performing the serial killer and doctor, John Bodkin Adams, about whom there were many conflicting testimonies – some testifying to his devotion and kindness, others to his extraordinary callousness:

> They say that truth is stranger than fiction but this is the sort of profound paradox that playing a real person can offer up and it's an extraordinary and highly stimulating test of your ability.

One of the major problems about developing more precise acting vocabularies is that among actors there is no common agreement on the meaning of words – to list just a few: 'impersonation', 'imitation', 'impression', 'enactment', 'embodiment' and 'incarnation'. Individual actors use terms interchangeably and fluidly. Descriptive languages are both scientific and abstract, and our discovery is the same as Goodall's – that 'where stage presence is concerned there is no getting away from the strange and uncanny.'[21] As detailed as the interviews are in their accounts of technique, strategy and reflection, they are also shot through with a discourse of mystery and mystique. Just as Goodall has done in her book, it seems very important to acknowledge the profound difficulty of the complexity of acting, and specifically the art of creating the presence of another recognisable, often iconic, figure. Goodall asks polemically whether actors are agents or conduits, mesmerists or hypnotists – and these interviews, as does Goodall's thesis on stage presence, reveal that these questions are too crudely formulated. The actors we interviewed think of themselves as agents and disciplined technicians, but, not surprisingly, there is much about their own creative process that they find tricky or impossible to communicate and there are things about the feelings they have in relation to the person they are playing that prompt them to reach for ethereal terminology. Callow has written that 'the embodiment of other people is black magic, the raising of spirits.'[22] Performing a real person feels like a form of illusory resurrection for an actor and as such, is, as Phillips puts it, even more 'spooky'. Others in this volume speak of how 'weird' or 'strange' or 'alchemical' it is to stare back at oneself in the mirror and to see the impression of a well-known face, living or dead. Phillips speaks of 'becoming someone else' when she played Dietrich; and West did not know how he arrived at such a precise stance for the composer, Beecham, and wonders quizzically about 'divine intervention' (though also says he had seen him perform once years earlier). In his autobiography, Antony Sher describes kneeling before a painting by Stanley Spencer in his dressing room on the first night he was playing him: 'I whispered a few words to Stanley Spencer, God Almighty, Jesus Christ, or whoever else was listening.' Like other artists, actors can be awed by their conscious and unconscious processes of creativity, especially in the moments just before they go on stage. But in addition to their technical powers something extraordinary can take place in the energies and expectations that move from performer to spectator and from spectator to performer at a live event.

Reflections

American and East European readers might find the few references to Stanislavski and other practitioners rather bemusing. Most of our

16 actors are British or trained in Britain. In the United Kingdom, mainstream actor training credentials do not tend to be defined by teachers, but by the professional parts an actor has played. British actors talk of parts they have played, whereas actors elsewhere in the world might talk extensively of the particular method they have been trained to use or the teacher who most influenced them. In Britain, there is a lingering distrust that theory can be useful in a practical arena, as well as a strong culture of belief that training is not only about the conservatoire but also to do with the experience of professional work. Readers may, however, recognise echoes of certain Stanislavskian exercises or Brechtian ideas behind what some actors say – but should be aware that none of these actors would describe themselves as purists, and all would argue that they have acquired different tools and techniques from different traditions and sources and that they deploy them differently according to the part. In time, and with a great deal more interview research, it should be possible to detect which particular practitioners are drawn on most for the playing of real people.

Space does not permit a lengthier introduction, but the three sections above do make it possible to outline common preoccupations. Playing a real person brings with it a specific sense of responsibility both towards the subject and the spectator. If the subject is a living person of significant influence, such as a politician, an actor's need to account for themselves and their representation is much more heightened than it would be for a fictional character. Playing a deceased person of note, particularly someone within living memory and/or of iconic status, also increases an actor's sense of responsibility towards their subject. The actor's need to be able to justify their portrayal to themselves seems to inform their process in terms of a commitment to exercising a greater control over his or her own ego or imagination – in other words, actors argue that they need to exert a certain kind of very disciplined focus which can serve to strip away extraneous detail that might distract from or distort a representation. In the case of the two actresses interviewed about verbatim roles, the pressures they talk of seemed to be overwhelming. What is of general note is the actors' concern that to exercise too much of their own imagination in the playing of a real person might simply be an inappropriate urge to indulge themselves, and that to exercise too little might risk a portrayal that lacks life and conviction.

Actors are acutely aware of their audiences when playing a person of note – whether direct relations or friends of their subject, or general public. Their representation must try to 'pass' both in terms of the images which have circulated in the public realm and in terms of the people who had an intimate acquaintance with their subject – yet the latter appears to be a particularly thankless, and not infrequently, impossible task. On the other hand, theatre audiences tend to 'read in' physical and gestural likeness and show a strong desire to believe that the actor's representation is accurate. A striking feature in the interviews is the actors' fascination with the paradoxical conundrum of the apparent knowability of someone who operates in the public realm and about whom there may be a great deal of information, and the actors' sense that their subject is irrefutably unknowable. With Stanislavski, background can be imaginatively filled in; with real people that background is often riddled with insoluble contradictions and inexplicable gaps of knowledge, which actors often feel it is not appropriate to obscure or neaten. These actors speak of a finely balanced combination of careful research and conjuration.

Notes

1. Michael Pennington, *The Guardian*, 26 November 2008.
2. Email to Mary Luckhurst, 13 March 2009.
3. Michael Sheen was very keen to give an interview for this book, but was always too busy playing real people.
4. Tom Cantrell is researching actors of documentary drama for a forthcoming book.
5. Mary Luckhurst is continuing research in this area for a future book.
6. Michael Sheen, Interview with James McClaren on *The Queen*, Radio Wales Arts Show, BBC Two Wales, 28 May 2006.
7. Frank Langella arrived at his portrayal of Richard Nixon in Peter Morgan's *Frost/Nixon* by 'watching him and watching him and watching him'. See: news.bbc.co.uk/1/hi/entertainment/oscars/7840832.stm (accessed 25 May 2009).
8. Callow, on the other hand, has described the moment when he found the route to playing Hitler in Brecht's *Arturo Ui* through a

'cheap joke shop false nose with a moustache attached'. Simon Callow, *Being an Actor* (London: Vintage, 2004), p. 185.

9. Helen Mirren, interview by Rebecca Murray. See: http://movies. about.com/od/thequeen/aqueen100406.htm (accessed 23 May 2009).

10. www.bbc.co.uk/wales/arts/sites/themes/film/michael_sheen_ frost_nixon.shtml (accessed 25 May 2009). In the same article, director Michael Grandage argues that Sheen 'dispenses with any impersonation' and gets 'deep, deep, deep inside' a person.

11. Interview with Rebecca Murray: http://movies.about.com/od/the queen/a/queen100406.htm (accessed 28 May 2009).

12. Chris Rojek, *Celebrity* (London: Reaktion Books, 2001), p. 77.

13. Callow, *Being an Actor*, p. 184.

14. See: http://news.bbc.co.uk/1/hi/entertainment/oscars/7840832. stm.

15. Mary Luckhurst and Jane Moody, eds, *Theatre and Celebrity in Britain, 1660–2000* (Basingstoke: Palgrave Macmillan, 2005); Joseph Roach, *It* (Ann Arbor: University of Michigan, 2007); Jane Goodall, *Stage Presence* (Abingdon: Routledge, 2008).

16. See Goodall, *Stage Presence*, pp.140–6.

17. Marlon Brando, *Songs My Mother Taught Me* (New York: Random House, 1994), p. 211.

18. Joseph Chaikin, *The Presence of the Actor* (New York: Theatre Communications Group, 1991), p. 141.

19. Ibid., p. 10.

20. Antony Sher, *Beside Myself: An Actor's Life* (London: Nick Hern, 2009), p. 219.

21. Goodall, *Stage Presence*, p. 10.

22. Callow, *Being an Actor*, p. 184.

Interviews

Roger Allam

Playing Adolf Hitler, Willy Brandt and Max Reinhardt

Roger Allam played Adolf Hitler in David Edgar's *Albert Speer* (National Theatre, 2000); the West German Chancellor Willy Brandt in Michael Frayn's *Democracy* (National Theatre, 2003); and the legendary theatre director Max Reinhardt in Michael Frayn's *Afterlife* (National Theatre, 2008).

Most stage treatments of Hitler have been parodic or comic in some way. David Edgar had anxieties that his portrayal of Hitler would be criticised by some precisely because he didn't want to use comedy to subvert the role. Did you have any worries about accepting the part?

It didn't concern me at all. The play is based on Gitta Sereny's book, *Albert Speer: His Battle with Truth*, which is all about Albert Speer's relationship with Hitler. To make Hitler some sort of monster would be wrong. He was seen by those in sympathy with his politics, by those close to him, as a powerful, charming and charismatic man and, to my mind, the whole idea was that you should see precisely that. You watch him selecting a kind of favourite who gets increasingly drawn in and his monstrosity is only revealed later, as Speer's opinions start to change and Germany's fortunes in the war decline.

To what extent were you involved in the creation of the role?

David tends to use rehearsals as a way of rethinking and rewriting and there was a lot of discussion, whereas with Michael Frayn that isn't the case at all. Everything is very finished: there might be one or two alterations but Michael attends at the beginning of rehearsals and then only comes again when we're running through.

Do you do a lot of preparation before rehearsals?

It entirely depends on the circumstances. Initially, I turned down playing Hitler because it coincided with the birth of my first son. Then, as my wife was going into labour, I got a phone call.

It sounds dramatic!

It was very dramatic. The contractions had already started! It was the director Trevor Nunn who begged me to do the role. He'd not been convinced by anyone else that he'd seen for the part and couldn't imagine anyone else but me doing it. Rehearsals were starting the next day. He was very persuasive. Anyway, I discussed it with my wife – we were having a home birth, you see, so it was easy to talk – and I ended up doing the play!

So there was no time for research!

I didn't have any time to do any pre-preparation but because I had come riding to the rescue, so to speak, and I had a new-born child at home I found I was in a commanding position! I delegated research tasks and instructed various assistants to get me all the DVDs and videos they could find and I asked David Edgar to give me a digest of books and articles to read. I found photographs helpful: there was one taken at Hitler's mountain residence in Berchtesgaden, where he was slumped far down in a chair and I stole that posture for a moment in the play. You steal anything that's useable really. I found the video material particularly helpful. Eva Braun's home movie material was the most enlightening because it showed Hitler in a private setting and in entirely different conditions from the public performances. I picked up certain physical mannerisms; for example, as commentators have remarked, he often stood with his hands clasped over his genitals. Home movies are useful because, whilst subjects aren't completely relaxed, you see another side to them. Obviously, you invent things as well. With the Austrian accent, for instance, I had the idea in my head that it might be slightly northern – it didn't come out that way, of course, but that's what I was imagining. You have to try and find a vocal equivalent. German is so explosive and it's a question of where the voice should be placed. His long silences in the play were important. He would be very physical, hold people and they would experience the sense of falling into his eyes – that was a very significant physical trait.

The abruptness of the process was quite liberating. It freed me from a certain responsibility. One can read too much and play the research rather than the role. I think I was perhaps more open to suggestion and I was happy to just dive in and try things out. This wouldn't have been possible if I'd been playing the protagonist, Speer, or if the play's title had been *Hitler*. If the play had been about Hitler, it would have been tremendously difficult to give a full reading of such a major role in such a small space of time, but in the play Hitler is only ever seen through Speer's eyes: you never see Hitler without Speer on stage.

Speer presents Hitler as a manipulator. Was that a factor in your interpretation?

I played Hitler completely sincerely. He totally believed in what he was doing. He was an idealist. Interestingly, he was also profoundly ignorant. Having read all the material I have, I'm not even sure how much detail he knew about the concentration camps. It seems that the Nazi regime worked like a sort of court. Hitler made pronouncements and his courtiers interpreted them and executed them for him. I'm not suggesting he didn't know about the camps, but he never visited them. He didn't watch footage. Unlike Stalin, he got no visceral pleasure from observing suffering and torment. He was squeamish. He didn't understand that by invading to the East to acquire the famous *Lebensraum*, he would vastly increase his 'Jewish problem'.

How do you play charm and charisma?

It's often about how others react to you. You also have to think about what your intention is, and what it is you are doing to those around you. If you do an actioning exercise and try to find your intention on each line you might have actions like 'I flatter you', 'I stroke you', 'I cajole you'.

Do you find actions for each line?

That's something I do only if I find that something isn't working. It's a useful way of analysing exactly what the character is doing at that moment.

What else was important to you in playing the role?

Being able to look in the mirror and think, yes, that passes for Hitler. That's very, very important. For one thing going out on stage you have to be convincing to the audience. Hitler consciously created a facial mask – bizarrely enough based on Charlie Chaplin. In a sense he was completely on the money because the face was instantly recognisable. When you're my age and you adopt a face that has haunted your entire childhood it's *very* weird. Finding a satisfactory way of resembling him was extremely important. I used my own hair which went dark when it was gelled. Once you have the hair and the moustache you're half way there but I noticed that his eyebrows were set lower than mine so I waxed out the top of my brows, keeping the middle and drawing them in lower, and the effect was really quite unsettling. Getting the eyes right made a big difference to me though I don't know that anyone in the audience would have noticed.

Did you have more time to prepare for playing Willy Brandt in Democracy?

I agonised for a long time about whether to accept the role. Initially, I thought the spy, Gunter Guillaume, who was employed by the Stasi – the East German secret police – and acted as one of Brandt's closest aides, was the plum part. He has all the fun! Guillaume's unmasking forced Brandt's resignation and became one of the great scandals in modern German politics. There wasn't a great deal of information about Brandt and West Germany in the 1970s and 80s. A very decent German social democratic leader doesn't tend to have so much written about him in English! Luckily I had material from Michael Frayn, there are a few books, and again there was useful footage and I studied his facial expressions closely. As I grew into the role I realised what a significant figure Brandt had been. His policy of *Ostpolitik*, of improving relations between the capitalist West and the communist East, was immensely far-sighted and progressive, and won him the Nobel Peace Prize in 1971.

The space you perform in also has ramifications for your approach to a part. I'd done Hitler at the Lyttelton, a large stage at the National Theatre with a capacity of nearly 900, but *Democracy* was produced on the small stage, the Cottesloe, which holds 400. The more intimate space led me to experiment with trying to get Willy Brandt's face with greater accuracy. I tried blotting out some of my hairline, I changed my eyebrows, I even tried a false nose at one point and it all looked *completely ridiculous*! It didn't look like anything other than someone wearing a great deal of make-up. In the end I tried to get a tone of voice with the right lilt, a very thoughtful tone of voice. He often had a furrowed brow, a rather perplexed look, which I used a lot.

What about mannerisms?

Brandt is a totally different case to Hitler. Hitler comes with a set of iconic visual characteristics and physical mannerisms, Brandt doesn't. Audience expectations for Hitler are both more clear-cut and more demanding than for a figure like Brandt. An actor in a recent German production chose to play Hitler without a moustache and I suppose he was trying to get behind the mask but, given that the mask is integral to Hitler's public persona, I wonder if this wasn't a rather indulgent experiment.

The process of doing Brandt was utterly different to Hitler. *Albert Speer* had a short run and was too expensive for a West End transfer, whereas I played Brandt for over a year – first at the Cottesloe, then at the Lyttelton, and then for six months in the West End. I never got bored with the role, even in the West End, where audiences found it a very demanding play.

What was it about the part that kept you fresh?

The very routine of performing it. I get irritable with actors who say they can't stand repetition because to me acting is repetition. It's fundamental to acting – the French word for rehearsals is 'repetitions'. Although acting is of a repetitious nature, that doesn't mean your performance is exactly the same from night to night. The act of repetition can also become rather contemplative. There's something very comforting about the routine of a long run. Life itself is so messy and unordered. If you're playing a role as satisfying as Willy Brandt, you have this piece of time where everything is more or less the same, which is reassuring. Backstage life is very ordered: there's a point where I might always have a cup of tea, or where a fellow actor is waiting in the wings with me, or where someone always says 'hello' to me, a half-hour where I go and wait in my dressing room. There's a kind of pattern to it which can become curiously comforting. I simply sank into the performing of the play. That may have also suited the character, I don't know. It was quite different to Tom Stoppard's *Arcadia*, where I discovered that all I could do was keep the part polished and shiny. The thing about a long run is that you've never finished with the part, there's always a detail to be honed.

What did you know of Brandt when you first read the play?

I remembered him when I was a child as Mayor of Berlin, with J. F. Kennedy at the Berlin Wall. Indeed, that was one of my early memories. I remembered him becoming Chancellor and his resignation under something of a cloud. I didn't know much more about him. I read about his youth, his introduction to left-wing politics, and his extraordinary facility with languages, as well as the different names and characters he adopted which was something that had caught Frayn's attention. I grew to really love him. Politically, he sought the language of reconciliation at a time when it was very, very difficult. He saw that reconciliation was utterly necessary. He seemed to me an honest, decent politician.

There's an extraordinary scene in the play where Brandt and Guillaume discuss the possibility that Guillaume is a spy. As an audience member you think, surely, surely Brandt knows what is going on.

I think in the play the character of Brandt loved the possibility that a communist East German spy might be one of his right-hand men. It becomes difficult to separate the real man from the invention of the play. Certainly Frayn delights in toying with the thought that Brandt might have relished the idea, but in reality I think Brandt the politician wouldn't have found any pleasure in it. In terms of the play, Gunter Guillaume's possible treason makes him more interesting to Brandt.

Late on in the play Brandt's sexual life is referred to and it comes as quite a surprise that he's clearly had extra-marital affairs.

Yes, the play doesn't explore the sexual side of his life at all. It's reminiscent of Kennedy's promiscuity and a sexuality of its time, I think. There's a tremendous physicality about Brandt, which is as far from Englishness as it gets. Two of the characters depicted in the play came to see the production, Horst Ehmke and Reinhard Wilke. They were wonderful! Horst was a powerfully built and impressive man, still very much a force in politics. He had his wife with him, an enormous Czech lady. They were so incredibly visceral and physical. They told filthy jokes the whole time. Whenever they told a joke about 'shagging', which was nearly every joke, it was accompanied by a vigorous pumping action with the right fist smacking the palm of the left hand. I used that gesture for the next few performances! It became a sort of private joke. There was something about their energy which was phenomenal. Horst's wife told me – and any double entendre was lost on her – 'You have the smell of Willy!'. They really loved the play.

You're playing Max Reinhardt at the moment, a person who many may not know anything about.

I studied drama at university so I knew of his significance as a modernist experimenter and the extraordinary epic productions that he directed, often involving casts of 1–2,000. He was born in 1873 and in the early part of the twentieth century he was an international celebrity, and directed and produced a phenomenal number of plays. He was a charismatic, larger-than-life entrepreneur with astonishing gifts and by the end of his life he'd built or rebuilt about 13 theatres. He's best known for his spectacular religious extravaganzas and for his world-famous production of *A Midsummer Night's Dream*, which he also made into a film starring James Cagney and Mickey Rooney. But there is a woeful ignorance of his significance as a theatrical innovator, very few know that he co-founded the Salzburg Festival, for example, or that he directed a production of *Everyman* each year. The part was offered to me quite a while ago, but again I took a long time to accept. The play is less a biography of Reinhardt than *Democracy* is of Willy Brandt.

Was it a difficult part to research?

It was difficult to get hold of material on Reinhardt. I got his son's book, which is very useful. It's often photographic material which is the most helpful. In the book there's a sequence of photos taken of him while he is directing: his reactions and responses are incredibly demonstrative and I was very struck by the power of his physical presence. I didn't know that he'd been an actor before he became a director so for him theatre was about the actors. That came as a bit of a surprise because he's always associated with extraordinary spectacle but then he also did productions of Strindberg's early chamber plays, Ibsen, and had eclectic tastes. He worked in many different styles, he didn't impose a concept on the play. Acting for him was not the Stanislavskian idea of immersing yourself in a character, but rather having a rich and interesting personality that engages with the material in the best possible way. I read about the difference between the theatre traditions in Vienna and Berlin. Vienna drew a great deal from Italy and *commedia dell'arte*, an acting tradition, which meant that it wasn't primarily a theatre of literature.

Frayn explores Reinhardt's love for Leopoldskron, the Baroque palace he acquired in Salzburg and spent years restoring before he was driven into exile by the Nazis.

Frayn meshes together Hugo von Hofmannsthal's play *Everyman*, in which God sends Death to summon a representative of mankind for judgment, with the narrative of Reinhardt's renovation of Leopoldskron and the exile forced on him by the Nazis because of his Jewish roots. I think the palace project was about Reinhardt's desire to make life and theatre merge together. In the play Reinhardt orchestrates the performance of life in a beautifully restored Baroque palace, but the project of restoration also destroys him. I remember an actor telling me ages ago that Diana Dors once said to him: 'If you're an actor and you suddenly make money, then it's very possible that you'll buy a large house.' I think that happens to a lot of people who have some success: they buy the big house and it becomes the thing they have to feed, it takes them over. It's interesting thinking about the poverty Reinhardt grew up in and the emphasis he came to place on owning beautiful objects.

How did you find a physicality for Reinhardt?

A few years ago I worked on David Harrower's *Blackbird* directed by the great Peter Stein. I loved working with Peter. He had a very visceral way of working. He was not intellectual. He wrestled the acting out of you. Everything that was done was examined, not dictated. You would get huge responses from him. He'd shout, 'No! No!' or 'Yes! Yes!' directly in front of you. Because it was a two-hander and we

had a six-week rehearsal period we had a great deal of his attention!
He was full of energy, wanting to act it with you. 'The body is doing
something different to the words', he'd remind us repeatedly. The
physical language was worked on in an extraordinarily detailed way.
He was wonderful. He wouldn't let anything get past him. I appreci-
ated it enormously. That experience with Stein gave me a way into
a culturally specific energy and physicality. I could connect those
photos of Reinhardt, so vigorously active as a director, with Stein's
appetite for the physical and visual. It's not that Reinhardt as a person is like Peter Stein but links have been made when Stein has done
his epic productions.

Which was the most difficult character to play?

In a certain way Brandt was the most difficult to play because it
seemed like a very passive role – you had to do a great deal of listening. It's easy to pull out a knife and stab someone, but to find the
way to listen is very exacting. You mustn't let your own ego get in
the way. I worry a good deal less about my acting than I used to. I've
learned to let go, as I said earlier, I've learned not to play my research,
not to try and direct the play. It's early in the run at the moment but
Reinhardt is difficult to play for other reasons. In the main the play
has been badly received and that doesn't help with confidence. Many
of the critics have disliked the rhyming couplets or the morality play
and in some cases both.

*Frayn seems more preoccupied with the play Everyman than with
Reinhardt.*

There's some truth in that. In a sense *Afterlife* itself is a morality play
and the depth of character isn't there in the same way as it was in
Democracy. In *Democracy* there is a kind of love story, a powerful narrative between Brandt and Guillaume, and that always helps the story
along with what could be seen to be dry politics. This is a very different play – it doesn't have a narrative of that kind in it. It's very
demanding because Reinhardt drives the entire play.

INTERVIEWED BY MARY LUCKHURST, LONDON,
25 JUNE 2008

Eileen Atkins

Playing Virginia Woolf and Elizabeth I

Eileen Atkins played Virginia Woolf in Patrick Garland's one-woman adaptation of *A Room of One's Own*, premiering in London in 1989, before playing for six months at Lamb's Theatre, Off Broadway, followed by several tours. In 1990 the production was filmed on location at Girton College, Cambridge (the venue of Woolf's original lecture). Atkins won all Off Broadway awards, including a Drama Desk Award for best solo performance and also received a special citation from the New York critics for her portrayal. She wrote and starred as Woolf in *Vita and Virginia* (London, 1993; New York, 1994–95), a play based on correspondence between Vita Sackville-West and Virginia Woolf. Atkins wrote the screenplay of Woolf's *Mrs Dalloway* (1997), which won the 1997 *Evening Standard* British Film Award for best screenplay. She also played Elizabeth I in Robert Bolt's play, *Vivat! Vivat Regina!* (1970, Chichester, West End and New York), for which she won a Drama Desk and Variety Award.

Where did your interest in Virginia Woolf come from?

My interest in her started in my late twenties. When I was about 27 or 28 I looked rather similar to her. I didn't as I got older, but at that age I did. I could see the similarity. A young man had a film script and he came to me and asked me to play her. I have to admit that at this point I hadn't read any of her work, but I thought the script was marvellous. Unfortunately the film never got made, but I started reading about her. I couldn't get on with *The Waves* at all, but I loved *Mrs Dalloway* and *To the Lighthouse*, and I suppose I got a bit immersed in her.

I came across the letters between Vita Sackville-West and Virginia Woolf and I thought that they would make a wonderful evening's entertainment, and that I could organise them into a shape and perform them at charity evenings instead of reading poetry. Sackville-West was an aristocratic writer and poet with whom Virginia had an affair in the late 1920s. Their letters make for fascinating reading. However, I found that even for charity you need the rights and I just couldn't get them. I couldn't get anywhere near either of the estates, and so I talked to a director friend of mine, Patrick Garland, and he told me that he was working on a one-woman show about Virginia. So Patrick and I did a deal: if I did a reading of his play *A Room of One's Own*, he would get me an introduction to the estates. *A Room of One's Own*, published in 1929, was an extended essay based on a series of lectures that Woolf gave in Newnham College and Girton College, Cambridge. It is a great piece of feminist writing. Patrick Garland adapted Woolf's lectures for the stage. I have to admit that at first I thought the one-woman show was rather dull and wouldn't last. I thought no one would want to sit through it, but I was quite wrong and it went on to be a smash hit. The Hampstead Theatre asked me to do it, then we took it into the West End, and then we went to Broadway. It got amazing reviews in America. However, I had been hoisted by my own petard in my deal with Patrick: because I was working for so long doing the one-woman show, I had to wait quite a few years before I had the opportunity to get *Vita and Virginia* off the ground.

So both plays started with readings?

They did, yes. I was not convinced at all but people were riveted by it. After the first reading I was driving home with my husband, who has nothing to do with the theatre and to be honest has sat through a lot of plays where he admitted to feeling bored. I said, 'thank goodness that's over', and he said that he had never seen anything so riveting in the theatre!

Playing a real person is very weird. I played Elizabeth I in *Vivat! Vivat Regina!* (1970) by Robert Bolt, which we performed in Chichester, London and Broadway. I won a Drama Desk and Variety Award for that. However, playing a historical figure such as Elizabeth I was quite different from Virginia. It was obviously far easier for me to find out more about Virginia because at least you could read her writings. For Elizabeth I, I just read about seven books about her. By doing this reading you encounter what I think is the big problem about playing real people. You read all the stuff about them, all the biographies and histories, but you have to remember that what you read about them has been made up by someone else. I'm not a great believer in biographies – I think people make things up to make their little idea work, to make it all fit in. So you read up, and then you come to this moment and all you have is the script and there is this danger that you keep telling the writer that from the research you have done you don't think she was like that, and that the writer should change how she appears in the play. In the end you have a dramatic script and that is what you have to make work. Often you have to let some of your favourite things about the person go, you can't bring them in. You can't argue too much with the writer, because you accepted the script in the first place and that is what you have to work with. But saying that, some of the things I found in the books about Queen Elizabeth were very helpful. Several of them said that she had the most amazing movement; that she had perfected the way of walking which made her look as though she was floating in those great panniered dresses. People described how she seemed to sail. That was a useful thing I could work on myself, without affecting the script.

I also believe in making an attempt to look like the person. I'm a great believer in make-up; in fact people were utterly astonished at the make-up for Elizabeth I. I didn't want to put on a false nose (both Virginia and Elizabeth had bigger noses than I have), I didn't want to do putty, I just didn't think it'd look right. I find it very odd these days that so many actors are against make-up on stage, because if you've got good lighting, I think it is very helpful. I went to one of the best make-up artists, and he had to see the lighting first, but he gave me amazing make-up. If you saw me offstage as Elizabeth I looked like a Zulu warrior – two very dark brown stripes down the side of my nose, which highlighted the middle, but with the theatre lighting it made my nose look much more strong and pointed. That really helped. I do believe in that deeply. With Virginia it was a little difficult because from the research I had done I found out that when she gave her lecture at Girton, the lecture that later became part of *A Room of One's Own*, she actually had just had almost all her hair cut off. She had a very bad Eton crop, like a 1920s bob. She was very unhappy with it, but that is how she looked when she went to Girton. When I first did it, I did it with cropped hair. People have their own idea of what she looked like, and to some extent you have to give in to people's preconceptions. The picture they have always seen is her with a bun. So in my most recent run of the play which was in 2001, as the final production at the old Hampstead Theatre, I did it with the bun. Things like that are interesting. It was the truth that she had short hair, but the public image of her was different. Balancing the audience's expectation with the actual facts is an interesting negotiation.

In addition, you obviously want to try and get the voice right. There is a recording of Virginia, but it was made at a time when recording was only in the very early stages, hardly anybody did it, and she seemed to speak very slowly and sedately, not as low as Vita Sackville-West – who is hilarious. There is a recording of Sackville-West reading a piece entitled 'Walking through Leaves' and it is terribly low and resonant. Virginia's voice is also much less posh than you would think, and much more free, but very slow. My conception of people who are very intellectual is that they tend to talk quite fast. That is my impression, and I think that it is the public's impression too. In the past, intellectual people also seemed to have articulated very precisely. There is something in their brain that is going at such a rate that they have to articulate quickly to get the thought out. But when I heard the recording of Virginia, I really did think that she couldn't possibly have talked like that all the time. I thought about it and I think that as it is her only broadcast, she was terrified. I bet lots of people gave her tips on how to do it. I'm none too sure whether that is how she actually spoke. So I tried to get the timbre, but when I actually perform I make her voice very precise and quite quick. It seems to me that a fast mind tends to talk fast. You see, one of the wonderful things about playing Virginia was that there were so many things said about her at the time by her contemporaries that I could read. By all accounts, from what I read she was a great chatterer. She can't have spoken like that and been a chatterer!

It certainly sounded like someone doing a recitation.

That's right. We have one recording. We can't presume at all that that is how she spoke all the time. It is very similar with biographies. We cannot presume that any are 'the' truth – they are all views, often based on one example. I am in about seven biographies, and often they try and characterise my personality by the way I acted one night. So when using biographies in preparation to play a real person, you have to take some license. You can't just follow everything that you hear and you read. I suppose it all comes down to the fact that as well as the externals, you have to somehow seek out the essence of the person.

So how did you start to find the essence of Virginia Woolf?

The diaries were a great help. I still dip into the diaries from time to time. You try and get into their way of thinking. Also, anyone who was as wryly funny as she was (or waspish if you are feeling nasty) must have been edgy and bitchy and fast. That is a particular type of person. You know the kind of movement that comes from those qualities. If you are in a room full of people and you know that one of them is bitching rather well, immediately there is an actual movement you can see. They usually don't sit forward, but lean back and it slides out. So that is what I mean by essence. I learnt about her personality and thought well if she is like that, I could observe someone today who is a bit like that, and see the physicality. Of course you have to be careful not just to play one aspect, lots of people went on about her bitchiness, but she was clearly more complex than that.

When I went to America with the show, we often had discussions after the performance, and I'd ask people what their thoughts had been about Virginia Woolf before they had seen it. Often, all they would say was that she was insane and committed suicide with stones in her pockets. But I really wanted to dispel the thought of her as a gloomy person. As a matter of fact very few suicide victims are gloomy. If they are manic depressives, you only see them when they are manic, they don't go out when they are depressive. They are often quite lively people. So never for a moment did I play the depressive, because it was not there in her writing.

I suppose I was lucky because the second thing I did, *Vita and Virginia*, was my own writing, so I had absolute control of what went in. I did include a little bit about her depression. If you are doing someone else's script, the worse thing in the world you can do is read too much because you come in and start arguing with the script.

Histories are hardly ever recorded truly anyway. What do they say about histories? 'It is written by the winners.' It isn't fact and how things were. An example is the opening of Antonia Fraser's book about Mary Stuart. She claims that she must have been six foot because of the size of the coffin. But as far as I remember, there was something about the contents of the coffin, and that they put many ceremonial things in, including her dog. Surely it is more likely that those objects would make it larger, rather than her being six foot, which would have been very unusual. So, you see, history keeps being rewritten. You can't look for hard facts – that is a futile exercise. Historians will always make their living from claiming something new.

Despite the fact that we have images of Virginia Woolf, I think there is a big difference between what I do and the work of someone like Michael Sheen, who I think is quite, quite brilliant. We know the people he is playing. Few people, if any, know that much about the people I played. If I had played Virginia in her own time, I would have given a very difference performance, I am sure, because I would be able to watch her. But I've never played anybody who is alive today.

How was it performing A Room of One's Own *at Girton College, where Virginia herself spoke?*

It was very funny. There were three old women still at Girton who had been to Virginia's original lecture. They were in their eighties. At first they said there was no way they were going to turn up to see some actress pretend to be her, but then their curiosity overcame them and they all turned up. They kept telling me how like her I was, and then afterwards one of them was questioned by someone else, not me, and they clearly could remember very little about her! In fact one of them remembered that it was a bit of a bore, that as students they had to listen to this boring woman! I suppose when you are 19 you don't really take in what someone is like.

You've said in previous interviews that you didn't consider your portrayal as an impersonation of her. What do you mean by that term, and how did your portrayal differ?

Well, I couldn't do an impersonation of her. I'm not an impersonator. Peter Sellers was an impersonator. People get very mixed up between actors and impersonators. So many people say, 'oh she ought to go on the stage, she does wonderful impersonations.' That is not acting. An impersonation is getting the exact voice, the exact look. It does so happen that some actors are brilliant impersonators – Anthony Hopkins is sensational. But if I had done the whole evening of *A Room of One's Own* in Virginia's voice, even discounting the radio voice we talked about, people wouldn't have stayed in their seats. You see she wouldn't have had the ability to change tone and rhythm in the way that actors do. It would have been a dull monotone probably, because that is the way that people who don't perform speak.

You also appeared in the film The Hours, *which was about Virginia Woolf. How did it feel working on the production?*

It was very hard for me. To me it destroyed the work that I had been trying to do. The ironic thing was that Michael Cunningham wrote *The Hours* after he had seen me in *A Room of One's Own*. He became interested in Virginia Woolf again, and had the idea for *The Hours*. I think it is a brilliant book, and then we had the movie, and I was asked to do one day on it. I think they thought it would be good to have me in on it, rather than criticise from the outside. I talked to them about how they were going to do Virginia's nose. I was in on the first day of filming and I asked make-up what they were going to do about it because Nicole Kidman has a little nose. The costume woman heard me say this and told me to tell the producers, so we did, and then they put that huge thing on her face. It wasn't right at all. It wasn't Kidman's fault, nor was it David Hare's (who wrote the screen-play) or Michael Cunningham's, but I was very disappointed as the only bit they showed of Virginia was her depressed and neurotic side. It was everything that I had tried to get away from. People used to come up to me all the time and say that they had no idea she was so funny, but of course that is why she was so popular. My work has been concerned with trying to show her gaiety, her fun, her wit. It tends to get forgotten and people just dwell on the mad genius.

TELEPHONE INTERVIEW BY TOM CANTRELL,
25 MARCH 2009

Simon Callow

*Playing Guy Burgess, King Charles II, Charles Dickens,
George Frideric Handel, Marcantonio Raimondi, Thomas
Cosway, John Mortimer, Wolfgang Amadeus Mozart, and
Oscar Wilde*

Simon Callow has played Charles Dickens on screen in *An Audience
with Charles Dickens* (TV, 1996); *Hans Christian Andersen: My Life as
a Fairy Tale* (TV, 2001); *Christmas Carol: The Movie* (2001) and *Doctor
Who: The Unquiet Dead* (BBC, 2005). He also performed the one-man
shows *The Mystery of Charles Dickens* (London and New York, 2000;
filmed in 2000) and *A Festival Dickens* (Edinburgh Festival, 2008). He
played George Frideric Handel in *Honour, Profit & Pleasure* (TV, 1985);
King Charles II in *England, My England* (Channel Four Films, 1995);
Mozart in the premiere of Peter Shaffer's *Amadeus* (National Theatre, 1979); Emmanuel Schikaneder in the film of *Amadeus* (1984);
Guy Burgess in *Single Spies* (1989); Thomas Cosway in *Jefferson in Paris*
(Merchant Ivory, 1994); Marcantonio Raimondi in *Cariani and the
Courtesans* (BBC, 1987); John Mortimer in *The Trials of Oz* and Oscar
Wilde in *The Judas Question* by David Hare (BBC Radio 3), and has
performed in *The Importance of Being Oscar* (Savoy Theatre, London,
1997), which is about Wilde.

How did your work on Dickens come about?

Someone working at a television company had the bright idea of me
recreating Dickens's readings. I thought I knew a lot about Dickens.
I had read a lot of his books and played Wilkins Micawber on television (*David Copperfield*, BBC, 1986) and I'd done *A Christmas Carol* in
rep, but like many people I didn't actually know that much about the
man himself. I certainly had no idea about how central his reading
tours were to his middle and later life. He spent many years touring

Britain and America, performing readings from his novels. It was an interesting challenge: to tell people the stories he told, and to perform them exactly as he had done them.

I decided quite early on, however, not to try to recreate his particular vocal habits. He had quite a high voice, a lot higher than mine, and he lisped. We know this because such was the popularity of his readings, wherever he went people transcribed everything he said phonetically. There were no recordings, but they took great pains to note down his voice according to pitch, and his vowel sounds – it was almost like musical notation. So it would be possible to totally reconstruct the way he spoke, but I couldn't see that it would be very helpful in actually reading the stories, where there was the additional challenge of portraying Dickens playing other characters. Although I was dressed up and made up to look like Dickens, I was aiming to be able to become his creations: Mrs Gamp, Ebenezer Scrooge, Mr Podsnap, which would have been very limiting had I tried to recreate his voice. We must also bear in mind that although he was a wonderful actor, he was not experienced, so his voice became frayed a lot of the time, and that was something I ardently did not want to reproduce. Very often at the beginning of a reading the back of the theatre couldn't hear him and he'd be quite voiceless at the end of a show. It was entirely exhausting for him. Again, we have detailed evidence for this. Dickens was one of the first human beings whose life was substantially documented. In his last tour of America in 1868, he had a doctor in the wings standing by all the time, and he took his heart rate before and after his performance; we have all the figures. The variation in the heart rate is alarming. So, in a way, recreating the reading is a very particular and specialist area in playing Dickens. One wants it to be truthful, but the primary loyalty is to the text – to telling the story he wrote, rather than his own story.

I played Dickens doing the readings again in book-ended, as it were, live-action scenes framing a very unsatisfactory cartoon version of *Christmas Carol* (*Christmas Carol: The Movie*, 2001), in which the principal character was a mouse. I finally got a chance to show a little of his life beyond standing on stage doing readings in a Hallmark film about *Hans Christian Andersen*, but it wasn't until the *Dr Who* episode that I got the opportunity of really showing something of what it might have been like to encounter him. Because of the time travel aspect, *Dr Who* has its own curious take on historical events and people. I had been terrified when they said that there is an episode of *Dr Who* where he meets Dickens, and would you like to play him, as I thought it might be a ghastly parody, but in the end I thought it was wonderful. The writer for my episode, *The Unquiet Dead* (2005), was Mark Gatiss, who is a real Dickensian. I think the episode was as good as *Shakespeare in Love* at giving younger people a flavour of what a writer and his era might have been like, but of course, even then, it cannot come close to showing his life in any depth. In all the manifestations of him I've played, there are always limits on how much we learn. I would love to play Dickens in a biopic if anyone would be brave enough to attempt one, though of course I'm already older than he was when he died. We are very different physical types: he was famously slight of build, and I'm famously not. But I understand something of his energy, which is the feature of him that all his contemporaries noted – that and his dazzling, infectious sense of comedy. He was a great performer in life, always 'on'. I suppose I can relate to that.

In The Mystery of Charles Dickens, *you don't play him.*

No I don't, I talk about him, I become his characters, but then increasingly towards the end, very gradually, I start to inhabit the older Dickens. The young Dickens fascinates me though. He must have been such a force of nature. It would be wonderful to have a crack at that. *The Mystery of Charles Dickens* is in a particular genre of playwriting, invented by the great Irish actor Micheál mac Liammóir, which I call 'living biography'. You talk about the character, you share what you know, you play the characters written by the author, and then eventually, as if you were operating some kind of Ouija board, you start to summon the actual person out of the ether. But even then, I continue to *talk about* Dickens. I only really become him at the very end of the play when I recreate his farewell speech at his last performance. Then I become him, speaking the words he spoke without quotation marks, as it were. It's just a glimpse of him, but placed where it is in the evening, it gives a slightly shocking sense of actually being in his presence. At least, I felt that when I was doing it. It is a rather particular performance style, I suppose.

I have returned to Dickens more than to anyone else, but I've played a number of artists of one sort or another throughout my career. I played the composers George Frideric Handel in *Honour, Profit & Pleasure* (TV, 1985) and Wolfgang Amadeus Mozart in Peter Shaffer's *Amadeus* (National Theatre, 1979), and the visual artists Marcantonio Raimondi in *Cariani and the Courtesans* (BBC, 1987) and Thomas Cosway in *Jefferson in Paris* (Merchant Ivory, 1994). I am neither a musician nor a painter, and it was necessary to learn something about their professional processes in order to be convincing, quite apart from their individual personalities. I spent a lot of time learning to play a tiny minuet of Mozart's in order to be convincing at the keyboard, but my hardest task was to convince the audience, as the director Peter Hall insisted, that I had written the Overture to *Le Nozze di Figaro*. In order to do so, I learned the music by heart, and spent whole days during rehearsals with it rattling through my brain, on the principle that Mozart must have done the same. Thomas Cosway was a miniaturist, the greatest of the eighteenth century, and I spent a long time trying to imagine what it is like to look at the world with a view to distilling and reducing it into that tiny oval. As for Raimondi, he was an engraver, so I did terrible, clumsy engravings of my own, but in the process learned exactly how he must have used his hands, and how disgustingly inky they always would have been. It helps to root you in a reality. The reality of what the character is. Then comes the question of who he is. Very often in a play or film, when you play someone who has lived, they cease to be themselves, and instead are adapted for the purposes of the drama. Very often when you do your research – you read the biographies and letters and look at the portraits – you realise that the character is infinitely more interesting than he is allowed to be in the script you've been given, which is hugely frustrating. It is the experience of many actors. You ask the director – 'could we not include this bit...' but necessarily it often has to be only one angle or dimension of the character which is being roped in to serve the film. So in *Amadeus*, Shaffer had created a very partial picture of Mozart. He made it very clear that it was Mozart as remembered by Salieri. What one had was a very stylised portrait. As an actor I still had to find a truth in it, the emotional context – you need to find the journey for the audience so as to keep them interested, but it is not a play based on a rounded depiction of Mozart. But this raises the central question: to what extent can you ever play a person that lived?

You can certainly capture their external mannerisms. We know quite a lot about the physical presence of King Charles II whom I played in *England, My England* (Channel Four Films, 1995), but in addition, in that case, one has the dimension of regality to contend with. Charles was a notoriously naughty monarch, but there was no doubt in his mind or anyone else's that he was the king. I must have succeeded to some extent in this aspect, because one day when we were filming in Greenwich Royal Naval College, I accidentally wandered off in full regalia into a section of the College where the public were admitted and ran straight into two American matrons who nearly had a heart-attack. They went into a half-curtsey, clearly baffled by the etiquette of how one behaves in the presence of a dead king.

In a sense, playing a person who lived, you almost have too much information. I think the key is to understand that any biography, let alone a film, is characterised by what it omits. So you try and sift through what you have learnt or observed for what is useful. You can learn a lot merely by observation. For example, I could do an impression of you – your accent, the way you look, the way you hold yourself, but I know nothing about your life, your family, your ambitions, and would be giving a very partial account of you, yet the tool of observation is a valuable one. When I'm directing, an exercise I often do is to get the actors to look at someone in the street during their lunch break and come back and play them. Just to see how much they can convey of another person from observation alone. Paintings – there are some wonderful representations of Dickens, particularly the cartoons – are immensely helpful. He was incredibly slight, small boned. They show his extraordinary eyes, emotive and penetrating. But I'm not any of these things, so I have to surrender to the principle of the character, try to find what it felt like to be him even though I can't really look like him. Voices are wonderfully helpful to me. When I played John Mortimer, whom I in no way resemble physically, I took the trouble to imitate his very striking, questioning, high-pitched voice, while adopting more or less his posture, and it really worked.

Acting is a curious, alchemical job. Another problem with playing real people is that most writers want them to make sense, but most actual people don't. The thing about Dickens, which is obviously true of any author or other artist an actor plays, is that we have their work.

The work came out of his brain, just as Mozart's music came out of his. In so far as I believe acting is essentially about thinking the thoughts of someone else, it is very important to realise that this was what was going through their mind.

When I was performing in *The Mystery of Charles Dickens* I felt that I changed my bearing when I was going to quote directly. I would try and capture a little of the dynamism of his performance. He half-humorously called himself 'the Inimitable' and said of his own performance 'bring on the bottled lightning!' – phrases like that are very suggestive – I think those descriptions were perhaps more useful than a picture or a letter in this instance.

Did you have a specific approach to playing Dickens?

There is a phrase invented by the Russian actor and teacher Michael Chekhov, 'psychological gesture', which means a gesture which crystallises the central essence of a character. It may not be a gesture that you actually perform, but it is key to your preparation. With Dickens, I developed a psychological gesture which was a bounding, bouncing quality – a forward movement. He was a committed walker – during his lecture tour he walked from Newcastle to Wolverhampton! That is when he was able to think about his writing, I think it freed his mind, he was free to dream. So I found a forward motion. I could feel that energy. I think the energy went through his life, whatever he did. If it was editing his magazines, he would be in the print galleys, in the compositor's rooms; he was obsessively busy and involved. So a way in would be to find in myself a feeling analogous to that.

Where did you come across Chekhov's work – was that part of your training?

No, I came to him later. I think he is the greatest of all the theorists. I place him higher than Stanislavski. Obviously he rides on the back of Stanislavski as we all do – we're saturated by Stanislavski in the same way we are by Freud or Marx. But Chekhov restored the innocence to acting, whereas Stanislavski deeply suspected actors. Stanislavski naturally presumed they were the way he felt he was – lazy, vain and inclined to fall into terrible habits. Chekhov, on the contrary, believed that actors, if allowed to connect imaginatively, could always contact the childish impulse to act. If you trust that, then almost everything is solved and you don't have to worry about it intellectually.

In The Mystery of Charles Dickens *you look briefly at Dickens's relationship with Ellen Ternan. The truth about the exact nature of their relationship remains unknown as they burnt each other's letters. Did you feel the need to make a concrete decision about their relationship?*

She was an obsession. She was absolutely the great relationship of his life. She, in a sense, became his next great project. You are right, the truth is we don't know. No one who was ever there when they were together has left any record of it. But you surmise – from the research I did I felt it could not be anything else than that she was his mistress. One is focused very much in *The Mystery of Charles Dickens* on moments of high drama, including Ternan, and also Dickens's relationship with his wife. They divided the bedroom in two, with a brick wall in the middle! So yes I made a decision for myself, from the research I had done.

This 'Living Biography' that mac Liammóir invented is a strange form. I love it. But of course there is so much left out. I have written two volumes so far on Orson Welles (*The Road to Xanadu*, 1995, and *Hello Americans*, 2007), which stretch to over a thousand pages, and there is no way I could digest that. Yet when I talk about Welles, about writing the book, and I recount his life, you still naturally find the most important moments in his life. Even in a work of over a thousand pages, it has to be selected highlights.

Are you tempted to perform a living biography of Orson Welles?

I don't think I would be physically qualified. I think if one were to do such a thing, one would have to really do an impression of Orson. I could possibly do it vocally, but physically I couldn't. But you see the great difference with Welles is that you would have to do the characters he played rather than the characters he created. So you couldn't interpret the characters as I could do with Dickens.

Before you performed as Dickens you played Wilde in The Importance of Being Oscar *(Savoy Theatre, London, 1997), how did that come about?*

When I was at University in Belfast in 1968, I was the dresser for Micheál mac Liammóir on the same show, so I knew it very well from the inside, but it wasn't until about 20 years later that I performed it. Then I had the problem that I had Michael's performance so strongly in my mind that I had to rid myself of that, but I think the Dickens piece is a better piece of writing. Peter Ackroyd is a great writer, not only with a deep knowledge of Dickens, but also he has a quality as a writer, as a biographer, to be possessed by his character. So one drew on that. As you know, in his book (*Dickens*, 1990) he has sequences between the chapters in which he talks to Dickens.

Did you and Peter Ackroyd work on the play together?

Yes. After *The Importance of Being Oscar* I wanted to do another show in the same form. The qualification was that the subject's life must be as interesting as his work – and that he must be British. I would love to play Honoré de Balzac, the French novelist and playwright. His life was wonderfully lurid and funny, but I don't think I'll be able to find anyone willing to write it. There is a superb modern biography of him; I went to meet the author, Graham Robb, and spent an afternoon wildly enthusing him with the idea, but by the time I got home, he had changed his mind! But with Dickens, over many, many meetings and many, many bottles of wine Peter and I discussed the idea. I told him how I believed the basic format should work, what the basic rules of this particular game were. A week later he had written the play. It was a complete disaster; so we had many more meetings and many more bottles of wine and three days later he had completely rewritten it. It was much closer, but still wasn't right. Then the following day, he delivered the play that became the working draft for the start of rehearsals. It changed many times throughout the rehearsals and then the run, I had quite a hand in the changes, we'd continue endlessly to play around with it. It was in the Australian leg of the tour, in Melbourne on the penultimate performance that I think it was finally perfect.

How did you choose which characters to play? Was this your choice or Peter's?

It would be a question, put crudely, of needing a joke here, or a vivid character here; it was more a question of shaping the piece. But through working on it, the notion slowly arrived that the focus should firmly be on Dickens and the theatre. Dickens being the writer

as actor. Everything about him is a performance. In the final production we had a scrim [a theatrical gauze which can appear solid or
transparent depending on which side is lit] behind which I sat, at the
very beginning. On the words 'the theatre!' the scrim would go up
and it was blazing with light and immediately we had the thrill of
the theatre, and I would go straight into something about Dickens in
the theatre ('What an actor you would have made, Mr Dickens', said a
stage hand at a gala in which he was taking part, 'if it hadn't been for
them *books*'). But originally Peter had a much more existential quote,
and that is the one that is in the filmed version of the show (released
in 2000): 'The more real the man the more genuine the actor.' Which
is a sort of puzzle line and you could tell the audience thought, 'well
I don't know what it means but it sounds deep' but it wasn't the right
first beat, so we moved away from that.

Are there specific demands of performing in a one-man show?

You need to find where the rests are; you need to map it tightly from
an emotional point of view. You have to get the energy from the material and the audience, those are your two allies. You can't let the ball
drop for a moment or it takes you half an hour to get it back up into
the air again. It is like a thriller, you've got to keep a question in the
audience's mind which intrigues them, keeps them wanting more.
One thing that changed through the course of the run was speed. In
the American and Australian leg of the tour I got incredibly quick. It
was almost as if, by the end, I would take a deep breath at the beginning of the play, and so would the audience, and we wouldn't exhale
until the end of the first act. It was a joy, but it was incredibly tiring.
A friend came to see it and he was very nice about it, but he said,
'Why? Why would you do this to yourself!?'

*You've played many artists and creative people. Do you feel through your
own work you have an understanding of these people particularly?*

I suppose yes, I do, as long as one acknowledges that what one is
doing is at a lower level. From childhood I always thought being
an artist was the most thrilling thing a human being could do.
I was never inspired by scientists or sportsmen. I was by lawyers, but
that's simply the theatrical element. I read biographies of artists –
writers, painters, actors – it was my way into the world. Therefore,

dealing with a biography of an artist is a natural choice for me now. At the moment I'm working with a young writer on a play about Tchaikovsky. This time it isn't living biography, but rather a conventional full-length play, with a full cast.

Portraying artists, writers and composers also raises the question about how you approach playing someone who is considered a genius.

It certainly does. You ask, what is genius? Can it be captured in a performance? I can't pretend to know. I've been around people whom I consider geniuses, such as Harold Pinter and Harrison Birtwistle. There is a huge pressure as your portrayal of them in the theatre needs to have the same impact on the audience that they did with people in life. That is a huge challenge. That was what was so brilliant about the *Dr Who* episode. Dickens was adored by everyone, they were in awe of him, and so I could play with that. Christopher Eccleston played the last scene brilliantly. I still find it terribly moving. Dickens says to him 'I have a question to ask'. 'What is it?', says the doctor, 'Will I still be read?', says Dickens. 'Yes', says the doctor. 'How long for?', 'For ever'. I thought those lines brought a fantastically human dimension to Dickens. But genius is an elusive thing to play. My portrayal of Dickens is part of an ongoing project in my life of celebrating great men. I've always been interested in the idea of greatness. Of what does it consist? My short books on Dickens and on Wilde both continue to explore this. But it is hard to grasp, and even harder to portray.

You performed in Edinburgh in 2008 in the same building as Dickens did himself.

I did, but I did the performances in a quite different way from Dickens. They were two stories, *Dr Marigold* and *Mr Chops, The Dwarf*, which we put together and called *A Festival Dickens*. These were monologues, or monodramas which he did as readings at a podium.

So he didn't learn them?

Well, he had really. It was all a trick, but he did it all with the illusion that he was reading. He had a frame, rather like a small arch which he invented himself, which had gas lights along it, to give the impression of a lit frame. It would be very interesting to reconstruct, but what I did in Edinburgh was completely different. It was something he never did – I dressed as the characters, as these pieces are drawn from what he wrote for *Household Words*, which are first-person narratives. So I played Dr Marigold, the travelling salesman and Magsman, the music hall director. I did them as two completely different characters. In fact, I'm going to do some more of those and revive all that, there are five such stories that Dickens wrote. But that was tiring, it was more tiring than doing *The Mystery of Charles Dickens*. *Dr Marigold* is one of his greatest stories. It really is blazing genius from beginning to end. Performing these you get inhabited by Dickens, and yet in *The Mystery of Charles Dickens* there were always periods when I could go back to narrative and calm everything down, calm myself down. I would have a moment of recovery, whereas these are relentless. Anyone who comes into contact with Dickens finds they are both warmed and energised by him but also exhausted by him. In *The Mystery of Charles Dickens*, I go some way to recreating his performance of the death of Nancy from *Oliver Twist*. When he performed it on stage, people thought he had lost control. It seems to be somehow associated with his wife, and that he was beating Kate to death. People in the audience fainted. I couldn't go all the way with that as I wasn't playing Dickens doing it, I was describing him playing it, but it must have been terrifying.

The first play you did was An Audience with Charles Dickens. *Did that turn into* The Mystery of Charles Dickens?

No, that was on the television (though performed in front of a live audience). It was the thing that started me on the whole journey. I did about eight readings on two consecutive Christmases. They were reconstructions of Dickens's readings. I was dressed as Charles Dickens in the theatre, there was an audience, and I spoke them from memory, but had the books to consult.

So you are going to return to the monologues. Is that in Edinburgh?

Yes, I am, but it will be in the West End. They are fabulous pieces of writing. They were hugely popular during his own time. There is a wonderful one called *The Boy at Mugby Junction* which is a satire on catering on the railways, which is in turn a satire on the whole English attitude to food, and then the English attitude to life. The other is *Mrs Lirriper's Lodgings* which is almost Joycean in its stream of consciousness. She really is Mrs Dickens, Charles's mother Elizabeth. Dickens wrote it during his work on his major novels, this was just what he did on his days off! He gave them to other people to continue, so the second episode of *Mrs Lirriper* is written by Mrs Gaskill, Wilkie Collins wrote one, and then Dickens wrote the last one.

He is the most fecund genius. More than Shakespeare as far as we know. We only know that Shakespeare wrote 37 plays. But Dickens was making speeches up and down the country, and even more amazingly, it is all documented. He was such a celebrity. Possibility the first celebrity in the modern sense of the word.

INTERVIEWED BY TOM CANTRELL, LONDON,
8 JANUARY 2009

Chipo Chung

Playing China Keitetsi, Nadira Alieva and Condoleezza Rice

Chipo Chung played ex-child soldier and activist China Keitetsi and Nadira Alieva, partner of ex-diplomat Craig Murray in Out of Joint's production, *Talking to Terrorists* (2005), directed by Max Stafford-Clark and written by Robin Soans. She also played Condoleezza Rice in Jonathan Holmes's play, *Fallujah*, in 2007.

How did you begin working on Talking to Terrorists?

I think Max was interested in having me as an actor because of my background – I come from Zimbabwe and I have a personal relationship with the material in the play because my parents were involved in the Liberation Struggle. The conflicts that China, who was a child soldier in Uganda, talks about are therefore very close to home for me. I think the fact that I could engage with China was what interested Max about me. Max really does choose actors carefully – they have to be keen researchers and have an intellectual interest in the area they are researching. So for me working with Out of Joint, Stafford-Clark's production company, was very much a homecoming – to a group of people who are workers for social change and I found that wonderful.

In many ways *Talking to Terrorists* is based on the work of Scilla Elworthy. Scilla is a huge agent for social change, and set up an organisation called Peace Direct, which mediates in conflict zones, trying to find non-militaristic resolutions based on facilitating dialogue between countries and organisations. She also runs the Oxford Research Group, which is an activist group identifying countries that support nuclear armament and she develops peace talks and discussion groups with them. Max and Scilla have known each other for years, and he became interested in her work. Max has a long-standing interest in documentary and verbatim plays. We started working on *Talking to Terrorists* whilst his production of David Hare's documentary play about the privatisation of the railways, *The Permanent Way* (2003), was running at the National Theatre. The cast, writer and director of *Talking to Terrorists* interviewed people who had been involved in violent change and had either come to a point of reconciliation or found a different way to be agents; those are the sort of people Scilla is connected with.

I was involved right from the beginning of the process. We had a short workshop at the Out of Joint rehearsal rooms about a year before the play was finally staged. At this point Max only really had the concept that he wanted to interview some of Scilla's contacts about 'terrorist' acts and construct a play from those interviews. With verbatim, everything is constructed from other people's testimony and for me that makes it very exciting. The play includes interviews with five people who in the past had been connected with terrorist acts: the individual I played, China Keitetsi, who is an ex-child soldier with the National Resistance Army in Uganda; ex-members of both the Irish Republican Army and the Ulster Volunteer Force; an ex-head of the Al Aqsa Martyrs Brigade, Bethlehem; and an ex-member of the Kurdish Workers Party. With Max and Robin, the cast also conducted interviews with other people affected by terrorism, either in their private lives or professionally, including politicians, diplomats, a psychiatrist, a journalist and an aid worker. We interviewed the ex-Ambassador of Uzbekistan, Craig Murray, and his partner Nadira (whom I played) about their experiences.

For the first workshop we had a group of actors, many of whom had worked with Stafford-Clark on *The Permanent Way*. I was one of only three actors from the first workshop to appear in the final production. Many of the actors in the workshop were used to the way in which Max involved actors in the research and development of the script, an approach that he's been developing since his work with Joint Stock in the 1970s.

Did you interview the individuals during the workshop?

Yes, many people. I remember very clearly the darkest day of the workshop was when a lady from Save the Children, who was played by Catherine Russell, spoke to us. She was very reserved, very closed, very centred and wary of what we wanted of her. We were all slightly devastated afterwards, not from anything she'd said but because there was something behind her eyes that suggested the experiences she had witnessed through her work. Actor Ian Redford and I also travelled to a military base in Wiltshire to interview an army colonel. It was great to see his place of work and then come back and basically explain the whole trip. I suppose we were functioning like journalists, constantly writing extensive notes.

In the interview itself, you'd be writing a lot of notes and asking very particular questions, and then we'd report back to the company. We would sit in front of the rest of the cast and the creative team and we'd still be reading from our notes, but re-enacting the interview at the same time. It is a technique Max often uses. He'd get us to re-enact and report simultaneously so that we would both be playing them and exploring different aspects of the character.

When did you first meet the people you were going to play?

I did meet Nadira, but I didn't meet China. Max and Robin travelled to Denmark to interview China, and I wasn't able to go. I was quite, not devastated by it, but quite disappointed. It gives you a huge hook to the character to meet them. You feel a great weight of responsibility as an actor in this kind of process. Firstly, you are concerned with the level of authenticity, but there's also a direct level of representation and obviously there's the director's view of it, which is also subjective. I felt a great weight of responsibility to be accurate. The main difference was that Max and Robin wanted an accurate rendition of the external aspects of the person in interview, whereas I wanted to give a sympathetic representation that China would like, which is not necessarily the same thing.

Were you given anything to assist you to compensate for not meeting China?

I read China's book, *Child Soldier: Fighting for my Life* (Souvenir Press, 2004). I didn't have any recordings of her and could only really go on what Max described, which is quite difficult as an actor, because you're not supported by knowing what you're aiming for yourself. For example, there was a point in her interview where Max told me that China got very upset – she was telling a story about when she was a child and she was beaten by her father. I wanted to establish what was going on internally to make her upset at that point, but the text really didn't help me. Max and Robin were very determined that at this point – you know actors always really hate this – they said 'at this point she cried'. On most parts you can work out your own interpretation and emotional journey, but here they said 'this is how she did it'. Obviously they encouraged interpretation and as I had never met her there was no mimicry going on, but they were quite pedantic about the fact that she did certain things at certain times. I found that very difficult, it would have been much easier had I met her I think, but I suppose then you have the added danger of mimicry.

The question of mimicry is very interesting in relation to verbatim plays.

It is. I played the American ex-Secretary of State, Condoleezza Rice, in another verbatim play, *Fallujah* in 2007. That was interesting because she is a public figure who is recognisable as opposed to China, who is not well known. But China and I do come from similar backgrounds. I wasn't a child soldier obviously, but I did spend my infant years in refugee camps, so there's a sort of personal resonance there for me. Therefore, to some extent one can get away with using one's own experiences, but with someone like Condoleezza Rice, who's a recognised figure, it is much more difficult. I'm 20 years younger than her, so that was an interesting acting piece for me.

I'm very interested in the voice, so there was some mimicry of her voice and some mimicry of her facial expressions and gestures and they did my hair like hers. At no point was it a deep Stanislavskian analysis of Condoleezza Rice. What was fascinating was that although I felt my work on the character had been so basic, people were absolutely convinced that I was exactly like her. Someone told me, 'I thought it was Condoleezza Rice that came on stage', and she genuinely meant it, and I thought, 'Hmm, it's just pulling a few funny faces.' You see, people project onto a figure that they know. If they can recognise certain gestures and similarities, they think it must be so complicated, but it isn't really. I think it is a magic kind of meeting place because it's a projected image; it's partly the audience's work, they have invented it. They want you to be like the person, so they believe you are.

What were your experiences of playing Nadira?

I was very pleased to be able to talk to Nadira in *Talking to Terrorists*, particularly as I felt that there were ethical issues in representing her. She is a belly dancer, and has performed in a one-woman reality play about her life called *The British Ambassador's Belly Dancer* (Arcola Theatre, 2008). On the surface of things, she's an Eastern European survivor who was a belly dancer in a seedy nightclub and worked her way into the British Embassy and managed to get immigration status here. She was with the ex-British Ambassador while his relationship with his wife disintegrated, which is not very good PR on the surface of things. But when I met her and I heard her story – she came from a very poverty stricken background, had to feed her family – that's why she was working in a belly dancing club. Her childhood was in a police state where young girls are sent into custody and raped and she'd experienced this many times, but in *Talking to Terrorists* the story of her hardship was very under-explained – why she had done the things she'd done. She'd experienced many horrible things at a much younger age than I was, and I found her very impressive; she'd escaped the horrors of her background. She clearly had a strange but genuine love for Craig Murray. It was very important to me – and I know people can be overly precious about their characters and one has to be interested in drama – that I didn't disrespect her while exploiting her story for personal gain. Verbatim presents real ethical conundrums: some people who came to share their stories were media savvy and knew how to manage their public persona, but people like Nadira are unused to public forums and the way their stories might be handled. I think one has to be careful. I'm sure that this was one reason why the woman from Save the Children was so defensive. She was guarding herself because she had no idea how she would be represented, and what our agenda was.

How did Talking to Terrorists *feel in performance?*

Throughout the run, from start to finish, it was in many ways the most restrictive play I have ever been in. There are plays that are written for actors and you grow with them and find different ways of doing things, and have a certain freedom too, whereas this was creatively very restricted. Much of the acting was direct address to the audience which means, as you're not acting opposite someone, you don't have their energy to use in a dramatic exchange. You have to keep to your little map. Also, the general acting note was less, less, less, to make it as super-real as possible. There was no room for thespian enthusiasm and largesse. Actors want to, as Max would say, 'twinkle': they want to twinkle and shine, and display their virtuosity. *Talking to Terrorists* was restrictive because we couldn't do that, we had to concentrate on the details of the story. However, the feedback from the play was that the acting was brilliant. I think documentary calls for more restraint in one's acting: the less outward theatricality you display, the more you serve the representation of the person you are playing. It is harder work, less fun than fiction definitely, and very exacting. There's a very high level of focus and concentration. It is not perhaps so much the responsibility of playing the part, as the writer's and director's insistence on direct address that made it restricting. The next play I did with Max was *The Overwhelming* (2006), which similarly was based on real events, but is a fictional play. We had greater creative freedom to use our emotions, but in *Talking to Terrorists*, and in documentary in general, you have to use a much more controlled emotional spectrum.

TELEPHONE INTERVIEW BY TOM CANTRELL,
7 MARCH 2008

Oliver Ford Davies

Playing Philip Larkin, John Ogdon, Charles Darwin and Oliver Cromwell

Oliver Ford Davies played Philip Larkin in *Larkin with Women* (Scarborough and London, 1999); the composer John Ogdon in *Virtuoso* (Ipswich, 1996); Charles Darwin in *Darwin in Malibu* (Hampstead, London, 2004) and Oliver Cromwell in his own play, *King Cromwell* (Orange Tree, London, 2003).

How did your involvement in Larkin with Women *come about?*

In 1999 I was asked by the director Alan Strachan if I would play Philip Larkin in a new play by Ben Brown at the Stephen Joseph Theatre in Scarborough. When I later asked him who else had been on his list he said I was his first and only choice. What this says about my perceived affinity with Larkin I hesitate to analyse.

Like many of my generation I had bought Larkin's two final books of poetry, *The Whitsun Weddings* (1964) and *High Windows* (1974), so I had a working knowledge of his writing. I had also seen two remarkable BBC *Omnibus* documentaries, which contained among much else fascinating footage of his visiting a church with John Betjeman. I then found there was a great deal more to read beside the poetry: his two novels *Jill* (1946) and *A Girl in Winter* (1947); *Required Writing: Miscellaneous Pieces 1955–1982* (1983); Andrew Motion's biography *Philip Larkin: A Writer's Life* (1993); and *Selected Letters 1940–1985*, edited by Anthony Thwaite (1992). I gorged myself on all this: my brief period as a university history lecturer makes me love the research aspect of being an actor. Alan Strachan also sent me tapes of Larkin

reading his poetry and, most valuable of all, his *Desert Island Discs* –
valuable because an unscripted interview reveals so much about character and voice (Larkin hated the interview and refused to listen to it
when it went out, another helpful character note). Since Larkin is
never offstage in the two-hour play, I had two-thirds learnt the part
before rehearsals started, so by the first day I was pretty comprehen-
sively prepared! My only further research was to visit Hull University
Library and talk to the current librarian, while studying the rather
grand room that Larkin had designed for himself. I also drove to the
two houses that Larkin had lived in and stared for a long time at
the outsides, conscious that Monica Jones, his companion of over 30
years, was still living in the second. I thought of knocking on the
door, but my courage failed me – perhaps in retrospect a pity.

The play covered about 30 years of his life, from aged 33 to 63
(1955–85). Since I was 59 at the time I was very much at the upper
end, but fortunately Larkin looked quite middle-aged in his thirties.
The core of the play was his relationship with three women: Monica
Jones, Maeve Brennan, a fellow librarian and his most 'romantic'
attachment, and Betty Mackereth, his secretary and confidante. All
three women were still alive in 1999, and had read the play and
vetted it, though we never discovered what Monica, a very acerbic
critic, really thought of it. We knew that Maeve had concerns that the
play might present Larkin too unsympathetically, or perhaps that the
actor might do a hatchet job on him. These misgivings were blown
up by the media and gave the production some notoriety, both wel-
come and unwelcome – it ensured that most of the first-string critics
came to the first night, editors sensing a possible scandal. Monica
was too ill to attend the play, but Maeve and Betty came and apparently enjoyed it. Maeve in fact saw it three times and became quite a
devotee, forming a friendship with Suzy Aitchison who played her.

*Larkin had a very distinctive appearance. Was it important for you to
capture the way he looked?*

Though I am tall and balding I don't look very much like Larkin.
I have a round face, while Larkin's was long and oval, similar, as
he himself admitted, to Eric Morecambe. We decided, however, that
I should try to look something like him, and once I had dyed my
hair dark brown (black is too tricky a dye for someone with fair hair)

and adopted his heavy, black-rimmed glasses the impersonation was passable. The voice was a different matter. I listened to the tapes constantly and achieved quite a reasonable imitation – I am not a gifted mimic. The snag was that Larkin's natural delivery was rather slow and uninflected, not good for stage purposes, and I finally jettisoned his accent and used my own lugubrious register which contained just a hint of Larkin. It is worth noting that Tom Courtenay, in his later one-man show, made by his own cheerful admission no attempt to look or sound like Larkin, while Hugh Bonneville, in a television rip-off of the play, adopted a quite accurate accent.

I approached rehearsing the part with some fears. We were performing it close to Hull, where so many people remembered him. More insidiously, since the publication of the letters in 1992, Larkin had been branded in many quarters as a conservative misogynist and racist – and indeed if you cherry pick the letters there are instances of both. He and his friend Kingsley Amis tried in their letters to outdo one another in reactionary sentiments; Larkin's perceived racism is usually quite mild (objections to the noise Pakistani spectators made at cricket matches); and I would describe Larkin as more misanthropic than misogynist (he had many female friends and championed various women writers, especially Barbara Pym whom he had never even met). The reasons for his cynicism and depressions are not hard to find. When he was a teenager in the 1930s his father was an admirer of National Socialism, and one school friend described the home he grew up in as 'joyless'. Though he was an Oxford first he hid himself away as a provincial librarian, finally settling in Hull, which he relished for its remoteness. He was often unhappy, began to drink too much, lost the ability to write in his last years, and his death from cancer at 63 was premature. Yet all those who knew him well, both men and women, testify to his kindness, dedication and great sense of fun. He was an intellectual who capered about to trad jazz, a contradictory character to squeeze into a two-hour play.

Larkin with Women is primarily a comedy, with much of the dialogue based on Larkin's own letters. Clive James wrote that Larkin was at times as funny as Woody Allen (when refusing the poet laureateship Larkin told Amis, 'the thought of being the cause of Ted Hughes being buried in Westminster Abbey is hard to live with'). There were, however, darker moments, and the final hospital scene (largely based on fact) where the dying Larkin is visited by all three women was very moving. Scene changes were accompanied by excerpts from his poems, which I had pre-recorded, and I found the continual reminder of his ability to pin down and illuminate a moment, a thought, an emotion, an enormous help. I read onstage the first verse of his last great poem *Aubade*, and I found this at times unbearable. There were of course those who thought the play and my performance sanitised Larkin – 'nothing about his racism', 'he was far more of a bastard to women' – but those who had known him found it a very fair portrayal. Certainly my impression of this flawed but talented man was greatly enhanced by studying and playing him, and I think it is precisely the contradictions and ambiguities in his character that audiences responded to. I have continued to work on his poems, and have given recitals of both his work alone and also linked to Thomas Hardy, his great influence. What is remarkable is that his reputation as a poet has dipped very little in the past 30 years. He is continually quoted in the media, and many writers, including the novelist Ian McEwan, testify to the great influence he has had on them.

You also played the pianist and composer John Ogdon in Virtuoso. *How did you become involved in the production?*

I was interviewed and subsequently offered the part in 1995 by Caroline Smith, a director I had never worked for. The play *Virtuoso* was to be presented at the Wolsey Theatre, Ipswich, in February 1996, with the possibility of a regional tour afterwards. After John Ogdon's death in 1989 his widow Brenda Lucas Ogdon had written, with Michael Kerr, a biography, *Virtuoso*. On the basis of this William Humble had written a television play, starring Alfred Molina and Alison Steadman, which played to great success. Humble had now turned it into a stage play, with considerable changes involving Ogdon's mental breakdown, visits to a psychiatrist and early relationship with his family – a more expressionistic take on the subject. I had watched the television play with great interest, and already knew something of Ogdon's phenomenal talent (he had won the 1962 Tchaikowsky prize in Moscow along with Vladimir Ashkenazy).

Ogdon's character was barely off the stage, and as we only had three weeks rehearsal the part needed a lot of preparation. I had to mime playing the piano to recordings of Ogdon, and since I don't play at all, I insisted that the most I could achieve was to have my arms moving to the right place on the keyboard, even if my fingering was inaccurate. I had four long sessions with a concert pianist, 'learning' some difficult stuff – the opening of Rachmaninov 2, Liszt 1 and Beethoven's *Appassionata*, and a tricky new work by a Dutch composer. I was sent tapes of Ogdon in interview, and after a lot of work I could give a reasonable imitation of his slight Lancashire accent. As the part was so long, and at times his speech so fragmented, I also spent a month learning it. All this work is of course unpaid, and not compensated by a large fee (the whole engagement yielded me less than £2000).

At our first read-through Brenda Lucas Ogdon was present, and we discovered that in return for allowing Humble to use her book as source material she had it written into her contract that she could attend any rehearsal (and presumably comment). Diane Fletcher, who was playing Brenda, found this particularly daunting as it was well known that Brenda had thought the television portrayal of her somewhat unsympathetic. As a result Diane felt obliged to give as sympathetic a portrayal of Brenda as she could – something of a limitation on artistic freedom of choice. We did, however, have a number of discussions with Brenda and found her very helpful and encouraging. To be able to talk to someone who knew the person intimately is a huge advantage, if only to be reassured one is not making drastically wrong choices. Brenda advised me, for example, on how little John moved his body when playing, and commented, 'you don't have pianist's fingers [...] which is good as neither did John'.

As John's bear-like presence was very distinctive, we knew I had to attempt to look like him. In fact the shape of my face and nose are very similar to his, and by the time I had put on heavy padding, a dark curly wig, his unusual tufted chin beard, and large dark-rimmed glasses, the transformation was pretty complete. When Brenda first saw me onstage at the technical dress rehearsal, she confessed it gave her a profound shock. It's hard to overestimate how important it is to feel you look like the subject. It not only boosts your confidence, it persuades you or, more probably, kids you that something of him is coursing through you. As you first step before the audience you need to feel that they will accept you as a plausible representation of the person in question.

Ogdon suffered a mental breakdown in his late thirties, almost certainly manic depressive (bipolar). As a near relation of mine had also suffered in this way and I had read books on the subject, I already knew a certain amount about the way it affected thought, speech and movement. Heavy drugs make it hard to stand still, for example, the feet are constantly shuffling, and I worked hard on this. A therapist at a local psychiatric hospital wrote to me during the run: 'Your portrayal of a mentally ill man was so realistic as to be (almost) boring to me [...] the hands and feet gave everything away'.

It was a very rewarding part to play, though extremely difficult. In one scene I was smoking, taking swigs of whisky, talking manically and 'playing' a particularly difficult piece of new music – all at the same time. The run of the play was only three weeks and on the press night the centre of Ipswich was gridlocked by a heavy fall of snow. The critics of *The Times* and *Independent* managed the journey and gave it good notices. The tour never materialised: the producer told me few theatres had shown interest in a half-forgotten pianist having a mental breakdown. In the end only a few thousand people saw the production. My daughter still maintains it's the best performance I've ever given. Such is the lottery and impermanence of theatre. One may give a lack-lustre performance in a play that runs in London for a year, and do one's best work in a play that runs for three weeks in Ipswich.

You also played Darwin in Darwin in Malibu *by Crispin Whittell (Hampstead Theatre, 2004). How much research did you do for playing such a famous figure?*

The play is set in the present with the deceased Darwin, perhaps in some parallel universe above Malibu beach, being visited by his old sparring partners, Thomas Huxley and Samuel Wilberforce. I look somewhat like Darwin, so beyond growing a beard it wasn't necessary to resemble a Victorian sage. Again I enjoyed the research. I read a couple of biographies of Darwin and also *On the Origin of Species*, which is fortunately a fairly easy read – and of course exciting beyond measure. But the greatest help was a visit to Down House, where he lived for the last 40 years of his life. His study has been kept exactly as he left it, full of the instruments of his research. Intent as he was on his work, he allowed his many children to burst in if they were in need of 'string, pins, scissors, stamps, rulers or hammers'. To be able to visualise such a detail is worth hours of reading. The gardens and greenhouses, where he carried out his botanical research, are also preserved, but most eloquent of all is the Sandwalk. This path round the grounds is where he did much of his thinking, and pacing this I felt as close to Darwin as I was going to get.

Finally you played Oliver Cromwell in King Cromwell *(Orange Tree Theatre, Richmond, 2003), a play that you wrote. What was it about Cromwell that prompted you to write the play?*

I had written plays before, and had had a few done on stage, television and radio in the 1970s. I think all actors and directors should try writing drama: it makes one so aware of the structural and conceptual problems a dramatist faces. The more Shakespeare I do, the more I appreciate the choices he makes, both daring and rash, and the more I find it informs my acting.

As I was out of work in the early 1990s I thought, since I had once taught seventeenth-century history, I ought to have a bash at writing a historical play. For some time I tinkered with a vast sweep 1642–60, but it always seemed to read like a pageant, so I went to the opposite extreme and tried doing a 'one day in the life of'. In the 1970s there was a reaction against writing about 'great' historical figures and the smoke-filled corridors of power. Caryl Churchill, Howard Barker and others rightly thought it was time to look at society from the bottom up. However, there is also a place for examining the people making political decisions, and here the most obvious candidate was Oliver Cromwell.

In 1657, Parliament offered Cromwell the crown. He hesitated for six weeks, then refused (nobody can be entirely certain why), and this I decided to telescope into one day. The 1650s is a particularly difficult period to assess, and used to be written off as a boring interval between the 'glamour' of the civil wars and the restoration of the monarchy. In fact the democratic revolution of 1649 (centuries before America, France and Russia) is of enormous interest, highlighting and rehearsing so many later global problems: how does a military coup find a democratic basis, how can you institute a non-hereditary presidency, how far can you extend freedom of worship etc. Cromwell struggled with all the issues from scratch, the writings of Rousseau and Paine were still to come.

Cromwell I am convinced is a very English figure, being both radical and conservative, like so many politicians after him. Professor

Blair Worden, perhaps the leading current historian of the period, saw the play and told me he was in broad agreement with my assessment of Cromwell, so perhaps my nine years of rewriting was justified!

How much research did this require?

A huge amount, both about Cromwell and the period in general. We have some rather brief letters by Cromwell, and rough transcripts of his immense, rambling addresses to Parliament, in which he struggles to make sense of what he's doing. He is an enigmatic, contradictory figure (always good for drama). He maintained a belief in elected parliaments – but not ones that disagreed with him. He wanted freedom of worship (except for Roman Catholics) – but had no idea how to achieve this. He was also very fond of music – in the home, not in church – and so I devised a kind of comic subplot concerning his reaction to the first English opera, *The Siege of Rhodes*, presented privately by William Davenant in 1657. This involved more research in the British Library, where I eventually stumbled across Davenant's libretto, which secondary sources had claimed was lost. I also visited the Cromwell Museum in Huntingdon, and we had a cast outing to his Ely home, which brought home his very provincial, agricultural background.

Were your concerns as a writer of a real person different to those as an actor?

The actor is given a text to work from, the writer is given a blank sheet of paper. The actor has to be wary of playing things that are not suggested by the dramatist (if Emilia plays that she is in love with Othello that could be very confusing, though for the writer it might be an interesting choice). When I played Larkin I tried to get the writer to include more about Larkin's mother, which I thought was crucial. The writer disagreed and so there was no way I could play this. The fiction writer has almost limitless possibilities, the biographical writer is more circumscribed but still has a dauntingly wide area of choice. The writer feels a responsibility to the person he or she is trying to serve. The actor shares this, but also feels a responsibility to the text.

In what way is playing a real person different from playing a fictional character?

The parameters are different. King Lear can be a tough old bull who should never have abdicated, or a frail man in the early stages of dementia – the text will support both readings. But with Napoleon you can't take such extreme positions – we and the audience know too much about him. With a modern part, Margaret Thatcher, say, the choices are even more limited. Nevertheless you still have some latitude. In all drama the actor tries to understand and inhabit the character's point of view (Iago had been passed over for promotion, Thatcher had to fight very tough male competition), but also to stand outside and apply a certain objectivity (Iago's response was disproportionate, Thatcher rashly let capitalism rip). The public self may be something of a mask, and dramatists often concentrate on the private person. The actor may have leeway to carry this further. Provided you do enough to convince or reassure the audience (perhaps in the opening ten minutes) that in appearance and manner you have some right to claim you are the real person, you can then pursue your own private take on the character, provided you don't wilfully misrepresent the facts of the text. Whether the actor feels a greater responsibility to a real person is a vexed question. Some believe that all biography is essentially fiction, others that playing a real person does require a response of greater integrity.

RESPONSES TO QUESTIONS SENT VIA EMAIL,
29 APRIL 2009

Diane Fletcher

Playing Clare Short

Diane Fletcher played the popular ex-Labour MP Clare Short in *Called to Account* (Tricycle Theatre, 2007), edited by Richard Norton-Taylor and directed by Nicolas Kent.

Called to Account *was a verbatim play performed at the Tricycle Theatre. How did you come to be involved?*

The Tricycle Theatre in Kilburn, North London, is a small theatre which has gained an international reputation for verbatim theatre. To date there have been six so-called 'tribunal plays', covering many contemporary political issues. All the previous tribunal plays, and this is where *Called to Account* differs, are based on inquiries into court cases. The writer on all of them, Richard Norton-Taylor, who is also a political journalist for *The Guardian*, edits the transcripts from the inquiries. Nothing is invented, but he condenses them for the stage. Past plays have included *The Colour of Justice* (1999), which Richard edited from the inquiry into the murder of Stephen Lawrence; *Bloody Sunday* (2005), from the Saville Inquiry into the killings in Derry in 1972; and *Justifying War* (2003), from the Hutton Inquiry into the suicide of Dr David Kelly. *Called to Account* focused on the legitimacy of the war in Iraq which began in 2003, and explored whether Tony Blair should be tried as a war criminal for misleading the public about the reasons for the invasion: it was different from the others as it was not a public inquiry. Instead the director, Nicolas Kent, arranged for two lawyers, acting for the defence and prosecution, to interview a range of people about the war. The interviewees included politicians, a weapons inspector, diplomats – a whole range of experts. I was cast to play Clare Short.

How did the process start?

At the beginning I was quite loath to accept the role. I have to admit the prospect frightened me – particularly the responsibility of playing her. I hadn't encountered anything like it before. I'd never thought of myself as an impersonator, or imitating – I'd never attempted it. The first thing that happened was that Nicolas Kent sent me the full interview with Clare Short on DVD. Receiving that terrified me even more! It was a very full interview, over two hours long. Obviously the final version was edited right down, which meant we had to lose lots of stuff that I was very sad about. Clare says in the interview she had been promised that a peace initiative in the Arab–Israel conflict, called the 'road map', would be ongoing and she would serve a better purpose by remaining in the cabinet to see it through. When this was shelved she resigned and felt used. At the time of the play she was still a member of the Labour Party, but she also resigned that post shortly after and now sits as an Independent MP. Most of what she said in the interview I also read in her book, *An Honourable Deception? New Labour, Iraq, and the Misuse of Power* (Free Press, 2004). I was horrified at the original length of the interview – because of the difficulty of learning so much. Though I was saddened by some of the important points in the interview that had to be lost.

We had three weeks of rehearsals. The play is comprised of 11 interviews, so I was only on stage for a very short burst. I found the process quite a lonely experience because although we're a team, you go on stage on your own, apart from the actors playing the lawyers. You don't interact with any of the other interviewees in the play. I had to do a lot of work at home – I did a great deal of homework, and I would go for my call, then just try and go through it as well as I could.

Did your homework involve the DVD that you were given?

Something I have only realised now, and I think as actors we take it for granted, is the extent to which we use our powers of observation. I used to play the DVD over and over again, and watch and listen. I suppose I did my normal process backwards. I have always thought of myself as an actor who works out how the thought affects physicality, but here I had to do it the other way round: I had to work out what she was thinking from the way she was moving, which fascinated me.

Was there anything in particular you were looking for on the recording?

Both the voice and the physicality, but also the timing. I would listen to it, turn the sound off and then try to match my movement to her voice. I'd try to work out why she was saying something or making a particular gesture. That was the battle. Sometimes she said things and I hadn't a clue why she said it or why she smiled at a certain point. So occasionally I would have to copy her without knowing why she was acting the way she was. There was one particular bit where she mentioned Gordon Brown, and she slightly smirked and I couldn't fathom why. I don't think they were great pals at all, so perhaps she was laying the ground for 'he's just as bad as Blair', I don't know, so I just copied her doing it. The audience had to work it out in the same way I did.

It sounds quite different from a Stanislavskian route.

I couldn't allow myself interpretation, which is usually the critical role of the actor. I actually found it very tiring. Exhausting. I think everybody did. We had quite a short run, but I wouldn't have liked to have gone on doing it longer than I did.

Did you find any other footage of her in addition to the DVD that you were given?

I watched her a couple of times on television. I found her accent hard to capture. It has a tendency to shift. Sometimes it is very Birmingham, sometimes it is RP and sometimes it has a slight estuary sound. The pressure that came with playing her was that many of the people in the play are not well known: they are not famous, but obviously Clare Short is very recognisable to people in the United Kingdom. I really felt under pressure to pull it off, as people could judge me in a way they couldn't with the other actors.

You say that you'd never considered yourself an impersonator – is that the way you worked on it?

Not really, not in the end. At first I think it was. It took me a while to get my head around it. It didn't feel like acting, it was a different skill. But then I realised this is what actors do: we watch people and then we try and recreate them. I suppose the difference in this case was that I had just to be as accurate as possible because I felt she deserved it. I believed in what she was saying. I felt very responsible for her.

Did you feel that it was important to look like her?

Well, Nick and the designer, Polly Sullivan, wanted me to dye my hair, and I said no. I have fair hair, and I just didn't think it would look right. Very kindly, the National Theatre did up a wig for me as the Tricycle cannot run to a wig department. To me the wig was crucial. She has got that very dark Celtic hair. That's one of the most recognisable things about her. We also tried to copy her clothes, to get as near as we could. That was quite simple, it was just a black suit with a red pashmina.

How did the play feel in performance?

Oh, it was terrifying, it really was. It was like being a butterfly, I was just stuck there, and I always hoped the questions would spark off the answer. It was a feat of concentration for everyone. If you let your concentration waver at all, you were lost and you couldn't act your way out of it. You couldn't invent; you mustn't invent.

Did the detailed set demand a certain acting style?

We did talk about this. The set meticulously recreated the original interview room, down to the smallest detail. We even had the camcorder onstage that was used to record the interviews – to act as a reminder to the audience that these were real interviews. I had to adapt slightly what I had seen on the DVD. Short kept her eyes down for most of the interview. For the purposes of the theatre, for the theatricality of it, I had to lift my head a bit: she only looked at the person asking the question, or away and down, she was always remembering and trying to be very accurate. She was obviously aware that she could face legal problems for saying something untrue. So

I had to adapt my performance, otherwise the audience would never have seen my face.

Did that adaptation go as far as playing to the audience?

No, it didn't, but that is why I'm glad we stopped when we did, because my acting instincts were taking over. I started to play to the audience very slightly and I'd have to rein myself in. It required such intense concentration. It also makes me question whether it was a play. I would agree in the end that I was acting, in that I was using the skills I am trained to do, but I don't think it was a play because there was no creative end. I missed the creative freedom of a fictional play – as my performance had to be the same every night, nothing alters.

Did Clare Short come and see it?

Yes, she did. I made Nick promise very early on not to tell me when she was in. I met her afterwards and she was very kind and positive. I think politicians are quite different from actors. They are much more confident people. When I met her, Clare had a very strong and direct quality. I also had a strong sense of her honesty and integrity.

TELEPHONE INTERVIEW BY TOM CANTRELL,
25 JULY 2007

Henry Goodman

Playing Sigmund Freud and Roy Cohn

Henry Goodman played Sigmund Freud in Terry Johnson's *Hysteria* (Royal Court, 1993) and the notorious lawyer, Roy Cohn, in *Angels in America* by Tony Kushner (National Theatre, 1992).

Do you have a different relationship with a character who was/is a real person?

Definitely. You have to instinctively understand your own received impressions of that character. There are so many prescribed reactions that we have built into us or general social responses, takes on different people, whether famous or not. Many of our responses are deeply affected by the signals that come out of the media and all sorts of other more hidden elements. Once you start rehearsing a play, it seems to me that even if you don't have that overt, articulate debate with yourself (which I enjoy but which a lot of actors don't), you are forced through the process of rehearsal and discussion to notice the assumptions that you make and either affirm or challenge them. Every actor has to negotiate the politics of rehearsal, the egos, the quality of the writing and whether or not it resists analysis. So often authors will say: 'I've done all the research, this is my take, my distillation, I don't need you to do the research and I don't want you to.' To an extent, they have a point: what they are saying is, 'do *my* version of this distillation, *my* take.' What I've learned over the years is how to operate in the political environment of the rehearsal room, and how to assess the confidence of directors and writers. What you have to understand is that some people become frightened when actors do what they think of as a writer's or a director's job. That might sound strange. On the whole, the good ones are not afraid and sometimes a British director will send actors off to do their own research.

Did you undertake research on Freud?

I always do a lot of research – it liberates my instincts, suits my personality, my interests as an actor and it's vital to my understanding of a play and its characters. It's interesting to think about playing Freud because there was the general social and historical background and then there was Henry Goodman, the personal, individual me. Some actors are very unassuming and do not bring their background knowledge to the rehearsal room in overt ways. I was attuned to the history of Central Europe, to Vienna and the melting pot of the secession, to the richness of modernist art and music, to Weimar and twentieth-century Germany. My Jewish background made me aware and I personally had an interest in the subject matter. I need to do the research and I need it because I believe that *information breeds instinct* – a phrase I use a lot when I'm teaching students.

Can you expand on that idea?

Research liberates the creative instincts: you can't create a performance by reading books about things, but you can get assurance, comfort and support as well as new ideas for instincts that may have come to you from the script. Even when you're playing a real person the writer may have invented a view of this person: that view might be bold and against the public perceptions that you have absorbed. In reading around you can determine for yourself what constructions the author is conforming to or working against. You can fill in the gaps and glean information that can liberate your creative energy. Jeffrey Masson's huge and controversial volume on Freud, *The Assault on Truth* (1984), had already been caught up in legal action and caused a major stir, and it played an important part in Terry Johnson's decision to write the play, as well as his own experience of therapy and other things.

What direction does an actor go in first? Do I go into therapy to do the role? That's another matter and an enormous discussion in its own right. You've got to start and end with the play, but in this particular case it's rooted in a fantasy that comes out of absolute reality. In order to make sense of Salvador Dali's surreal visit to Freud, which is based on a real-life encounter between the two, I went to the theatrical intensity of Freud's nightmare at the end of the play. Information is encoded in the script, such as Freud's three sisters being taken off to a concentration camp. I read up on the background to Freud's life and as a result his character became more emotionally charged and much more powerful in my imagination. The concentration camps are only implied in the play, but that history is absolutely laid out in Peter Gay's biography, *Freud: A Life for our Times* (1998), which I found very helpful. I was playing an 82-year-old man who was dying. The thing that liberated my imagination was reading about all Freud's early struggles in Vienna with Fliess, the other doctor.

The play turns on the idea that Freud may have lied about his original theory of sexuality. Although the play opens with Freud as an 82-year-old man, coping with remarkable events, a man who escaped from Germany and then from Austria, the fulcrum of the play is centred on events much, much earlier in his life. It's also what Freud's theories are all about, that we are all informed by deeply seminal events in the first five years of our life. Masson accuses Freud of lying about his theory of infantile sexuality, of hiding his real feelings because he had allegedly indulged in incest. By reading around the cases that came to Freud as a young doctor in his twenties, I was able to find the inspiration to play him as an old man. I was fascinated by his great intellectual gift, of course, but also by the notion that he must have carried a profound guilt for years and years about his sisters' terrible fate. If Masson is right, then did he also live in denial, did he lie to himself? I read essays by Freud. I read *Moses and Monotheism* (1939), which is mentioned in the play. I read David Stafford-Clark's book *What Freud Really Said* (1967) because it distils his theoretical positions and I was, after all, playing *the* expert on analysis. I didn't discuss this to any great degree with the director or my colleagues, that's to do with the politics of rehearsal and sensitivity to one's colleagues, but all this research gave me enormous strength and conviction in the creation of the role. *Hysteria* presents a minefield in terms of research and to play Freud effectively I needed to have an understanding of many things: making assumptions on the basis of a rough grasp wouldn't have provided me with creative fuel. So

I informed myself about the political, social and artistic worlds of that time, about psychoanalysis, the fight with Jung, about Viennese society and its surface decency, German history and the concentration camps. Without doing all that work I wouldn't have been able to understand how charged these things were in Freud's psyche.

I came to understand through the play and my background reading that something about Viennese life, Prussian life, at that time enforced repression. It seems to me nowhere better could someone have discovered infantile sexuality or hidden drives. That tension between the civility of everyday life and the multiplicity of yearnings, passions and needs hidden beneath is particularly open to a rich exploration in a surface, eloquent, well-mannered society. The research gave me an understanding of the tensions in the play but also meant that I was more sympathetic to some of the other characters, the women, for example. The play explores the repression of women and the manipulation of women by men, by Freud. Indeed, Johnson strongly attacks Freud's treatment of women.

How did you deal with the overturning of assumptions about Freud? Did you make a judgment on Freud?

This is really crucial. It's an obvious thing to say and everybody will say it to you: you can only act the play, not your view of your research. You have to submit to the text as an actor. That doesn't mean that you can't bring intuitive and imaginative ideas to the process of rehearsal, but the vision is Terry's and you have to serve the authorial instinct. I need to have sympathy with Freud. Every actor will tell you that it is vital to sympathise with the person you are playing. As Freud, I have to believe in the rightness of my actions. As Henry the actor, standing back, I can see that this play hinges on an argument but if I am going to experience Freud's guilt and discomfort, I can only do that if I understand that he's been lying or that he has been accused of lying and that the accusation really hurts. The play shows you brilliantly that Freud is living in a nightmare of guilt: the spectator doesn't know that until the end but, as the actor, I have to play it so that by the time we get to that insight it all makes sense. Terry has taken what you think you know and re-minted it. Freud was a man of incredible importance in the twentieth century, a great icon, an icon of intellectual discovery, but the play gives you an insight into tremendous emotional pain and internal chaos.

Did the idea of playing an icon make you nervous?

This isn't the same thing as Michael Sheen playing David Frost, where there was a lot of energy going into playing a current television personality. You can still hear Frost on radio and television. Freud died in 1939. There's a difference in the audience reaction according to the degree of currency of the person you're playing. When I played Freud, audiences weren't sitting there thinking: 'Did he get the voice right?' I did a lot of specialist research on the Austrian accent but what I am engaged in is not the same as someone like the impressionist, Rory Bremner – it's not brilliant mimicry. The fascinating thing was that as soon as I opened my mouth and started playing, people thought 'It's Freud! That's him – on stage!' I was repeatedly told that I looked just like Freud or sounded just like him, even though those audience members can't have had an immediate memory. Many had never heard the sound of Freud's voice nor seen footage of him and yet they thought my likeness to him was amazing. It's a sort of social memory, an 'icon memory'.

That's an intriguing concept.

It had a smell of authenticity about it and I'm not saying this out of vanity, but I hope that came about because of the all the hard work I'd put into it. So playing an icon didn't repress me, it liberated me. There were lots of things for me to soak up. I wasn't doing mimicry. I was trying to create intense intellectual concentration, for instance, the gift of someone who listens beneath the verbal exchanges as he's talking, because the dialogue Terry had written captured that. A different example would be Roy Cohn. He'd been dead six years by the time we did *Angels in America*. The play had a huge impact. It radically rethought the whole notion of a gay play about AIDS, and the state-of-the-nation play. I read a biography about Cohn which explored all the duplicities of his life and then I read his own autobiographical essays, and the difference was so startling that it was a wonderful liberation! The perception of what an outsider had written versus Cohn's perception of himself couldn't have contrasted more starkly. I was liberated by the thought that the guy is an out and out manipulative shit, not just because the play captured that and Kushner was interested in exploring him as a social phenomenon and symptom, but because of what Cohn had written about himself. To give you an example, I read in Cohn's writings: 'I was wearing my orange jacket' and I thought how many people, even in America, wear an orange jacket? That's a real clue to his extrovert nature and his vanity. It's details like that, the living with his mother, and other clues that give you very valuable insights. These details weren't in the play but they really stimulated my imagination and my understanding of him. You could do the play without all this research but the background work on real, living characters enables me to flesh out things that actually happened, the way people actually lived and it fires my creative intuition. That differentiation between what someone says about him or herself and what other people say about them is always absolutely fascinating.

There's a disclaimer at the beginning of the play by Kushner in regard to Cohn. Were there legal anxieties about representing Cohn at the time?

I know Tony Kushner was nervous, but I was never particularly aware of those dimensions. There was great fragility about the ambitiousness and boldness of the play. The concern was more about getting the balance between the political and social aspects of the debate about homosexuality and the flamboyance of the characters – we didn't want the characters to stand in the way of the political debate. There were, emotionally, a lot of tensions: people felt that they were given scenes that they couldn't quite handle. There was a closed rehearsal for the sex scenes, the buggery in Central Park, which we ended up performing ten feet apart from each other and it was the most ruthless rape scene you could imagine. Tony came in and instructed us on gay sex in Central Park, told us what happened and how – that's research too. It's important to stress that reading is only one kind of research used to fuel instincts which fill out experience. Reading is only a small part of research: some people do it by going deep inside themselves, by challenging their received opinions, rather than by reaching for books.

What did you know about Cohn before you read the script?

Nothing. I'd never heard of him. I didn't know about his nefarious dealings in the indictment of Ethel Rosenberg. I saw this fantastic role. It was quite clear, with the benefit of hindsight, that the research was coded in the play. Tony wasn't challenging public perception. When I read the biographies they absolutely supported the character in the play. The great thing that I keep coming back to is that in the playing of it – when I am inside the skin of Roy, I'm not Henry. I know it sounds a very simple thing to say, but it's a very far-reaching and crucial point: when Roy's sitting at a bar with a young man whom he wants to screw and manipulate in every sense, the electric dynamic of that scene is about an older man with a young, potential lay. That's what you are playing: he is what he is. Of course, I had lessons with an accent coach, I watched footage and heard recordings of Cohn – that goes without saying – but what gave me the confidence to go for it was detailed research and talking to Tony.

I'd say that there's less of an appetite for company research than there used to be. It's difficult to generalise but that's my experience. There are directors, as I've said, who encourage research but the English have an instinct for the division of labour. Directors, writers and actors do different things and worry about treading on each others' toes. At its worst, a director says: 'I know and you don't. Your job as an actor is to undergo experiences, my job is to know about the research that I've been doing for a year.' I've never subscribed to that view but sometimes the pragmatic reality of rehearsal politics insists upon that division of labour.

This may sound contradictory, but eventually the actor needs to be in a good state of *not* knowing. This isn't a state of ignorance, but rather innocence, a prepared openness to the starting point of the play. There has to be a readiness to divest, or to discard, then inhabit, imbibe from conscious work to unconscious work. Research fits into that cycle. You must never, never try to display your research; it must be in the service of the play. You have to be able to drink it in and then forget about it and either it plays in your mind or your instincts or it doesn't. It's a fatal mistake to try and act your research. To try to understand the social and political contexts of a play is, it seems to me, tremendously liberating. I'm not just talking about literacy. You might listen to relevant music of the time. It's about provoking, encouraging, filling out, so that you can more fully understand the scenes in the play. There is another side to research, however: it can be a very dangerous, messy business. You can discover things which are utterly unhelpful to your thought process and you have to know what to discard and filter out. Quite understandably some actors prefer not to do it because they fear getting into deep water, losing their clarity and focus, and so they prefer to rely on the director. I enjoy the research and I know how to distil it, but this isn't true for all actors. They might have read a wealth on the Russian Revolution but they don't know how to deploy their knowledge to help them play the scene. There is a skill in selecting and being open to that which is useful.

On this issue of playing real people I think it's important to pay attention to scope. The image of Shylock in today's Western cultures is that he's still walking down the street. He's living and breathing in everyday life. There's a cultural necessity for these 'others', these exiles and aliens to exist throughout the generations. Certain characters are emblematic, they are in the culture even if they are dead or 500 years old. They are wholly alive in another sense. In inheriting the role of Shylock I inherited Garrick's, Olivier's and Tony Sher's interpretations. I read all about their various takes on it, something that many actors definitely wouldn't do, but I'm interested in trying to understand the insights they had about playing that character – the impulse that they discovered in a moment of a script. They noticed something. A sense of history gives an actor a humility: it reminds us that many fine, fine actors have played the role in previous generations and moved audiences to tears. I don't mean you steal their stage business. Analysing the business, seeing where it comes from and what it relates to, is enormously informative. The first thing I do is read the play really thoroughly and have my own gut instincts which I often can't articulate. I enjoy the research because I find it enlightening. You smell out things. But I'd argue that a character such as Shylock carries the burden of a live reality as well. He's just as 'real' as Sigmund Freud or Roy Cohn.

INTERVIEW BY MARY LUCKHURST, LONDON,
20 MAY 2008

Jeremy Irons

Playing Harold Macmillan and Claus von Bülow

Jeremy Irons played the Conservative Prime Minister, Harold Macmillan, in *Never So Good* by Howard Brenton at the National Theatre (2008) and Claus von Bülow in *Reversal of Fortune* (1990), for which he won an Oscar.

Was the play completed when you became involved in Never So Good?

Yes, I received the play quite late. The first act was read at the National in November 2007 and they thought it was very good. The Artistic Director, Nick Hytner, had already planned the spring season, but thought that the play was very topical and should be produced as soon as possible, so the season was reshuffled to fit it in. I was contacted around Christmas, by which time the play was finished. In a sense, a play is only ever in draft form, though it altered very little during rehearsals – there were a couple of lines here and there. The production had to be pulled together very quickly. Howard Davies, the director, had a month to get the set design completed, normally that takes six months at the National.

What did you know about Macmillan before your involvement?

Not a lot. He was the first prime minister that I remember. Like many people I'd assumed he was a rather uninteresting old fogey. I was intrigued by the play when I received it because it's hardly what you'd expect from Howard Brenton. I wondered why this renowned socialist playwright had been compelled to write a play on a Conservative Prime Minister. Unexpectedly, I was immediately attracted to the character and the play taught me a lot about him. I realised that he's been seriously misunderstood by my generation. He'd be regarded as left-wing by current political standards.

His life was marked by astonishing events.

He had quite an extraordinary life. He was born in 1894 and died in 1986, he was wounded five times during the First World War and it was a miracle he survived: on the fifth occasion, he lay wounded for eight hours but dug himself in and famously read Aeschylus! He'd lived several lives before the age of 25. He successfully served Churchill during the Second World War and somehow avoided death in a plane crash in North Africa in 1943. He lived through the era of the Welfare State and the end of the Empire, and eventually became Prime Minister in 1957 as a result of the Suez Crisis, serving until 1963 when he was forced to resign because of a series of government scandals that ended with the Profumo Affair. Of course, there's a lot that isn't covered like the Nassau Agreement and the US's provision of the UK with nuclear missiles, the notorious spies Burgess and Maclean, and Macmillan's enormous house-building programme. It's the selected highlights of a career. But I think in the same way that *Henry V* is a great play and is not necessarily that accurate about Henry V, this is a great play but not comprehensive about Macmillan. It's not a documentary and the peripheral characters – the characters from his life – his wife Dorothy; Robert Boothby, with whom Dorothy had an affair; and Rab Butler, Macmillan's Home Secretary and later Deputy Prime Minister, get less attention. You know that some audience members would love to know more about those areas and those people but you can't cover everything. The writer has to make choices. I think the play gives you an overview of a long period in the twentieth century, a flavour of it, and of this man who happened to be there.

Did you do any research before the rehearsals?

Yes, I watched footage of him before the rehearsals began, and I continued my research during rehearsals. I found the video footage tremendously useful, as I did when I played Claus von Bülow. Howard Davies also gave most of the other actors projects to research – I was excused because of the amount of lines I had to learn. So the company members gave talks on their research back to the group, covering many different aspects of the period.

I also talked to people who had met Macmillan, such as his daughter-in-law. Pretty much all the people I spoke to had met him when he was the Earl of Stockton, the title he took from 1984 and when he really flowered. Since I have been playing him I've had letters from three of his secretaries who have seen the production. One wrote: 'I worked as secretary for Harold Macmillan from 1960–3, and you have captured the character of the man brilliantly. You took us on a remarkable trip down memory lane.' Another says: 'You brought him back to life. I worked with him when he was Foreign Secretary and also in his private offices of Whitehall before Anthony Eden moved into Number 10. When I was a young girl of nineteen I got transferred to Eden's office. His violent bursts of temper were so scary that on bad days I would dart to the loo when he rang his bell for secretarial assistance. So, Jeremy, you can imagine my worry that these memories that I cherish might have been a little shattered, but on the contrary it was a blast from the past. Macmillan's sense of humour was so well scripted. I remember he smiled a lot despite his teeth. He was sadly the last of the great elder statesmen.' I think she phrases that well. I've come to think that he was one of a dying breed of elder statesmen. So I spoke to people about him, but I decided not to talk to any politicians. I didn't need to really. I remember playing a surgeon in a David Cronenberg picture, *Dead Ringers*, and I said I must go and talk to some surgeons. Cronenberg said 'Don't, the star surgeons do it their own way.' Then he said 'You're going to wear red', and I said, 'Oh that's funny I thought they wore green.' 'Well, these wear red!', he replied. Sometimes, the reality of some professions is not useful.

So before rehearsals when you looked at the footage, were there any particular things that caught your attention?

I learnt he had a sense of humour, a twinkle in his eye. He was a little shy and rather humble. I was mainly struck by his dry wit. I'm finding his humour more and more. A lot of the time he is with Anthony Eden, who was famed for his temper, he is trying to diffuse the situation. Everything is in the play, what you have to do is see what the playwright has given you. Brenton has given Mac a spine through the play: he's dramatised two formative experiences: getting chucked out of Eton, and losing many of his friends in the First World War. Macmillan clearly felt, as many of the survivors did, that he was not worthy. I think these two events are hugely important. Brenton also devised a cleverly dramatic storytelling strategy by having both a Young Mac, played by Pip Carter, and an older Mac, played by me. It's a very effective way of exploring the importance of events in his youth. Pip is a wonderful actor. We didn't need to talk a great deal because he had an instinctive grasp of the part. The only thing I wanted Pip to do was to smoke in the trenches, which I never persuaded him to do because there wasn't time in the scene. I wanted it in because I knew Mac had smoked.

Did you make a decision about the question of his homosexuality at Eton?

For me there was no question about it: he admits the homosexuality at the end of the play. I think he had a schoolboy affair, it became known, he told someone who told someone else, and as a result of that the older boy was kicked out and ruined. But we don't know who the older boy was. So at 15, Macmillan, who was at his most tender age sexually, was removed from school. His mother's cover story was pneumonia, but your contemporaries know the real reason. It seems to me you then have a mother who has a hold over you. So it's no wonder that he didn't become the most amazing lothario like Duff Cooper, the MP and diplomat remembered for his playboy lifestyle, and that he wasn't a lot of use to Dorothy. He certainly put all his effort into his work, rather like Laurence Olivier in some ways. Added to that he lived with the knowledge that everyone knew Dorothy had a long-term affair (1929–35) with one of his colleagues. It battered his self-respect as a man. He dealt with it in a very English retiring way, but the agony induced a nervous breakdown.

Did you read Macmillan's diaries?

Howard Davies did, I didn't. You know there are six volumes! Howard prompted me with any relevant material. Howard Brenton was in the rehearsal room for about the first week, which was very helpful – if we ever had sticking points or problems we'd sit down and talk about them. I did read Duff Cooper's diaries, which are a much livelier read and give you a flavour of the period. Interestingly, Macmillan doesn't crop up much in Duff's diaries. He wasn't a bright star like

Duff Cooper or Anthony Eden, but he was the right man at the right time to see us through the Suez Crisis – even though it was sort of past his time.

How does it feel to be playing someone the audience recognise? Is it different from an invented character?

You have to be robustly persuasive from the start. In the first five minutes, you have to walk on and say: 'This is Macmillan. Forget what you know, or how I look – because I don't look like him. This is him.' You have to find his spirit. You find it by reading about what people say about him – it's rather like a crossword – you find clues and you begin to piece them together. But it's no different from playing somebody who isn't real, no different at all. You're trying to find the spirit of the character, what makes that character tick, what makes him what he is. You have to play the character as it is written in the play, and it is very difficult. Dorothy in real-life was nothing like the Dorothy invented by Brenton. Eden is nothing like we see him, well, perhaps elements are there, but it is not a fair summation of Eden. You have to portray what the play needs. It's the same with an adaptation of a book into a film, you have to make the character work for the film. You can't say, 'but in the book she's like this'. Film is a different medium.

Is your experience of playing Macmillan comparable with that of playing Von Bülow?

I definitely found I got into Macmillan more easily. Von Bülow was tried in America in 1982 for attempting to murder his wife. He got 30 years, but in a notorious appeal case was exonerated completely. He was harder to get into, mainly because I didn't like him very much. I like Macmillan a lot. For a long time I said I wouldn't play Claus. I watched him over and over in the court scenes and on three chat shows. I observed how he reacted to questions. I began to think, well, if my father had got himself into a terrible mess, I think he would have reacted just like that, with charm and good manners, and possibly an enigmatic quality. I'm very like my father, so maybe I would have reacted in that way. I got into that character through thinking about my father.

Did you grow to like Von Bülow?

No, looking back, no. At the time you don't think about that, as you are sitting there you don't think do I like myself? You know what you are, and you are what you know. You are too close to the character, but once you have left them you can look back at them. Mac I think I will always like. He is a very honourable man, a very sincere man. Very human. Not a superman.

You use the phrase 'once you have left them', is your habitation of a character just whilst you are on the stage?

No, I think once you are playing it, it is just on the stage – you slip that coat on. When I am rehearsing I think about them all the time. I'm constantly learning my lines and trying to work out meanings and why they say certain things. So that's the time I'm wrestling with a part, and that continues to a certain extent. We had a three-week break from *Never So Good* that finished last week, and when we came back one or two things that were new and fresh happened that hadn't happened before. Little details give us life. If a role isn't growing it is dying.

In the text Brenton emphasises the importance of Macmillan's 'ah'. He describes that it signifies moments of great betrayal.

I've never found his 'ah' in footage. Howard writes about this well-known 'ah' and I wish I knew about it!

In terms of physical resemblance or other traits, presumably there is a compromise – you don't look like him, but were there discussions about how much you should be made up?

Howard Davies left it up to me. I don't have much time backstage, and the epic range of the play is considerable so there are three looks I have, basically, and I cheat on the last one. I change the side of my parting, so it is on the same side he had. I try to make my hair do what his did, sometimes more successfully than others. I experimented with taping my eyes down so that they sag, and discovered it was not workable on a nightly basis, but I think it would be something I would do for film. I listened to his voice. I experimented with his walk – people used to say he'd slide across the floor because he didn't have good balance as a result of his war injuries – apparently he'd sometimes fall over in long grass and on uneven floors, so I worked out his physicality. I've seen pictures of him as a younger man, and so I take my wig off and use my own hair which behaves rather like his used to behave, it kind of flops. In the second act when he pulls himself together and decides to go for the top job, I cheat because he says earlier on that when he became Prime Minister, he grew his hair thicker and smartened himself up a bit, and I do that in the interval, just before he becomes Prime Minister as it is the only time I can do it. It just gives the look of someone who is beginning to grey, who has wings, and I hope those touches are going to be enough for the audience.

But you feel these aspects are more for the audience rather than an aid for you?

Oh, it does aid me. It's all part of the same thing. With Claus he was very, very thin on top so I emulated that. I got the voice – the right diction, and one hopes it is enough. I remember I saw George C. Scott play General George S. Patton Jr in *Patton*, and of course he doesn't look a bit like Patton at all, but after a couple of minutes on the screen you thought 'that's Patton'. That's all you have to do really. The audience suspend disbelief on a significant scale.

Do you think there is a difference in the suspension of disbelief between theatre and film?

Yes, I think I'd be more concerned with physical resemblance for film. It's much harder to lie to the camera. But in the theatre, people are further away from you. People tell me I've captured Macmillan's gestures fantastically. Of course, I don't know his gestures, but I do know that gestures come from what you are feeling. It's intuition.

Has any Prime Minister seen it?

I hear John Major came to see it. I think the politicians came very early on. I don't know if Maggie's been. I was speaking to David Davis, the Conservative MP, the other day and he'd certainly enjoyed it.

How did you approach playing Macmillan in the private scenes, when most of the footage is of the public world?

Well, everyone said he was a great showman in public, but I think he became a showman. I heard someone say they once heard him speak and he seemed not to be aware of where he was and what he was doing, until everyone was very nervous, and when he finally spoke he just blew them away. It's a very old trick – you make the audience worried that you are not up to it, and when the audience is on the edge of their seats, you hit them with it. There's not much opportunity for me to show the side of the showman, indeed that side is not very interesting. He was able to sell an idea, and he enjoyed all of that, but most of what we see in the play is the private side. He narrates himself in the play.

The first speech is one of the great contemporary openings!

It's a marvellous first line: 'I always had problems with my teeth' and it makes it clear that the play opens after his death. One thing I discovered is that Jeremy Irons doesn't do bad teeth! I thought about it, and talked to dentists about blackening them, but I decided against it. Macmillan was very self-conscious about his teeth and tried to conceal them by holding his top lip over them. It made him speak in a certain way, so I do the same which helps me find his voice.

How did you find the physical language of the different scenes?

We just experimented. Howard Davies had no ideas of how it was going to work. We just tried things. Suddenly he'd say, 'that's great', so you'd stick with that. Howard says the most important thing a director has to do in rehearsals is to remember what worked. We always worked from the text. We didn't improvise.

How do you think the role has evolved over the run?

It's very difficult for me to say. Roles can become too polished. You do them again and again, and you carve little patterns and you slow down, and you can lose the initial spark, because you become more and more conscious of what you're doing. I keep trying to change and develop. Timing is very important. At the end of each act I always ask how long it was, and last night we put on a minute in each act which is always a sign that you are slipping. So if we keep the timing right I can tell we're not getting too indulgent.

Do you enjoy having a run of this length?

I do, this has been one of the happiest productions I have ever done. I have a lot of other life, and because we are in rep and don't perform every day, I can juggle other things. It also helps that we aren't doing a relentless eight-performances a week, which is a killer. You are able to come back and see it afresh.

INTERVIEWED BY TOM CANTRELL AND
MARY LUCKHURST, LONDON,
24 JUNE 2008

Matthew Marsh

Playing Werner Heisenberg, Albie Sachs and President de Klerk

Matthew Marsh played Werner Heisenberg in the premiere of Michael Frayn's play, *Copenhagen* (National Theatre, 1998) and Albie Sachs in David Edgar's *The Jail Diaries of Albie Sachs* (Young Vic, 1984). He recently filmed *Endgame* for Daybreak Pictures in which he played ex-South African President Frederik Willem de Klerk.

Perhaps we can start with Copenhagen – *at what point did you become involved?*

I was asked to meet the director, Michael Blakemore, and Michael Frayn at the National Theatre about a month before rehearsals started. They had already offered the play to a very famous actor who didn't want to do it, for which I am eternally grateful. Michael Blakemore had seen me in an Arthur Miller play in the West End about four or five years before *Copenhagen*. I was sent the play, and I remember when I first read it I thought it was a masterpiece. It was one of those rare occasions when you feel really excited about working on a great play. And so I met them both and I was offered it. They took a gamble as I hadn't worked at the National before.

What did you know about the subject matter before you read the play?

Nothing. I don't think I'd even heard of Heisenberg's uncertainty principle. I failed every single science exam at school. But what excited me about the play is that it is as much about the relationship of three individuals as it is about science. It explores the world through the prism of science. Perhaps I should explain, the play focuses on a meeting between two leading nuclear physicists. My character, Werner Heisenberg (1901–1976) was German, and his colleague, Niels Bohr (1885–1962), was Danish. Both had been at the forefront of developing the new science of quantum physics during the 1920s and 30s. During the Second World War Germany occupied Denmark, and in 1941 Heisenberg visited Bohr. Posthumously, the play brings the two men together along with Bohr's wife, Margrethe, to try and establish the reason for Heisenberg's visit. The question about whether Heisenberg was assisting Hitler by researching the potential for an atomic bomb, or whether, in fact, he deliberately got his calculations wrong so as to stall progress has been hotly debated by historians and academics. Heisenberg is probably most famous for his uncertainty principle, which states that the act of looking at a quantum particle alters the velocity of the particle, and similarly that measuring the velocity alters the position. In short, the act of looking at a particle changes the behaviour of it. Frayn, then, uses the uncertainty principle and applies it to the actions of the characters in the play. The notion of 'uncertainty' is key.

Before rehearsals began were you told to read certain things to start to understand this?

We were pointed in the direction of particular books. I started reading the biography of Heisenberg by David Cassidy, *Uncertainty: The Life and Science of Werner Heisenberg* (1992). It contained a lot of very complicated science, but I read it up to the point of the Second World War, but after that line learning took over. I also read around about nuclear bombs – I read *The Making of the Atomic Bomb* (1986) by Richard Rhodes, a fascinating book which gives an overview of science in the first half of the twentieth century. I've continued to read the popular science books that have been published about it, which I find intriguing. I realised that there were scientific theories that were accessible to me.

Did you feel it was necessary to have a good understanding of the science to do the play?

Yes, I reached the level where I did understand the science as expressed in Frayn's speeches. If you asked me to explain it on a deeper, more scientific level, I would not be able to, but Frayn's writing is so clear and lucid and he has a knack of finding a way of explaining complex ideas. Of course this slightly diminishes them, but the essence of them is there. We spent certainly the first week and perhaps some of the second week of the rehearsal period reading and discussing the play. Michael Frayn was in for at least the first two weeks, so we could question him about the play and the arguments in it.

How did you feel about the fact that Heisenberg was a real person?

I think the simple answer to playing real people is that the better the quality of writing, the easier your job, and the closer it is to doing an entirely fictional play. With a fictitious play, all that you have to go on to instruct you is the dialogue in the play – what the playwright has included about your character, both in what they say themselves and what is said about them, and you build it all up from there. Sometimes you make instant decisions, and others you work out slowly in rehearsal. With a brilliantly written play like *Copenhagen*, I'd probably say you could play it without doing any research whatsoever. The higher the quality of the writing, the less research you have to do. However, if your character is very famous, your freedom for interpretation is reduced. With Heisenberg, whilst some people may have read about him and have some awareness of his physics, most people's knowledge, if any, would be sketchy.

Obviously one wants to try and find a degree of truth in the portrayal of a real person. I picked up certain useful things from his biography and other books, and also the way other people talked about him. What caught my attention was his incredibly fast mind, his boyish enthusiasm for things, he was slightly prone to be withdrawn sometimes, or could give the impression of rather overly imposing himself, he was naïve about certain things, he was a wonderful pianist, a fantastic skier, loved the open air, and perhaps had an innocent asexuality when he was young, but later got married and had children. So you pick up all sorts of things and you weave those in. Frayn did his research so well that everything you need is in the play. Heisenberg's son went to see the production in New York, and he said, 'I never saw my father get emotional about anything except when he was talking about music.' In this play Heisenberg gets very emotional at certain points, so in a sense perhaps that is a lie, but for a play to work you need drama. Similarly, Niels Bohr, apparently, was one of the most slow and rambling speakers you could ever meet, but you can't put that on stage. You have to find the balance between verisimilitude and the demands of an evening at the theatre.

The central question in the play is the discussion over what was said when the pair met in 1941. Did you need to make a decision about the purpose of Heisenberg's visit?

Well, we did the play for eight months at the National in repertory and then six months in the West End, and I was aware that through the course of the run my view changed. Perhaps it was an actor's desire for your character to be empathetic, but I wanted to give him as much benefit of the doubt as possible, so initially I worked on the assumption that he didn't want to build the bomb for Hitler. Then as we went through the run, I started to doubt my own reasons for thinking that. Clearly, the play contains the seeds of doubt, particularly in the things that Margrethe says. It was interesting, as although I had changed my opinion in my mind, I bet an audience watching me in both versions would not know the difference.

Is it important that your character is empathetic?

Assuming his innocence and playing that to the full gives the drama the chance of working. When the play begins, I don't think Heisenberg is thinking, 'I know exactly why I visited Bohr and I'm not going to own up', but that he is still wrestling with it – he is still ambivalent about his own reasons for visiting Bohr. Frayn's afterword is useful here, 'Thoughts and intentions, even one's own – perhaps one's own most of all – remain shifting and elusive. There is not one single thought or intention of any sort that can ever be precisely established.' It echoes the uncertainty principle. The same uncertainty applies to intention I think. I'm aware of moments from my life, moments of great drama, when I was in conflict with someone, for example, when I was absolutely certain of what my intention was at that time. But then six months, ten years later, you look back and think, 'oh no, my real intention was this...'. We think we understand ourselves but we don't and the play expresses this brilliantly.

Were you interested in his physical appearance, and what he sounded like?

We decided not to do accents, although some people have said to me since, 'your German accent was great', and I wasn't doing any accent at all. I had a formality in the way I spoke, which may have been construed as a German accent. I may have seen the odd clip of Heisenberg on film, but we certainly had lots of pictures and a lot of descriptions from contemporaries, which were very useful. When Heisenberg was the age at which I played him – about 40 – he had longish hair brushed back from his fringe, but I never attempted to mimic that. I suppose the other thing about *Copenhagen* which makes it different is that the characters come on at the beginning and say, 'now we're dead, we're ghosts, let's talk about it'. I think that gives you more licence in physical resemblance – you don't have to look identical.

I also played Albie Sachs, the legendary South African campaigner against apartheid, in David Edgar's play. You could not find a person that looks less like Albie Sachs. Albie is swarthy, with black hair, and skinny. At the time I had long floppy blonde hair. I looked like a blonde stormtrooper. David Edgar's play was based upon Sachs's actual diaries written in prison, so you are speaking words that he actually wrote, whereas Frayn has made them up. Albie was then blown up in 1987 or 88 by the South African secret police and lost an arm and went blind in one eye. David Edgar and the director, David Thacker, rang up various people who'd been in the production to do a benefit performance for him, and I played Albie again. We raised £20,000 that night, and Albie was there. So I played Albie in front of Albie. In his book, *The Soft Vengeance of a Freedom Fighter* (2000), he has written a chapter about watching himself portrayed on stage that evening.

What was that occasion like for you?

Oh I was shitting myself, but I really wanted to do it. I hadn't played it for four years and we only had three or four days' rehearsal, so it was all about getting through it.

I've just come back from filming a television drama, *Endgame*, in South Africa. I played Frederik Willem de Klerk, the ex-president, who famously helped engineer the end of apartheid. Albie is a small character in that film. But playing de Klerk is almost the opposite of *Copenhagen*. I had four or five little scenes at the end of the film about the secret negotiations between the ANC and the South African government, most of which took place in England in the last two years of the 1980s. Pieter Willem Botha had his stroke and then de Klerk took over. There is a lot of footage, so I watched that, I read his autobiography, and they put a bald wig on me because he was balding.

Are there differences in the demands of film and theatre when playing a real person?

On film and television there is more of a demand to be physically like the person when it comes to recent history. With de Klerk, I wasn't trying to do an impression or a caricature, but if you come on in a film and you are nothing like him, then you've got a problem. I've also played Elton John, believe it or not, in a television film. It was a TV film about John and Yoko. I don't even play the piano. I had to do a mimed concert in Elton's outfit and glasses – it had to be the Madison Square Gardens concert where John came and guested. There wasn't exactly much character exploration going on if I'm honest.

Does playing someone like de Klerk, whom the audience will recognise, feel like a different sort of challenge?

Playing a cameo role like de Klerk, there is no sweep of drama to get your teeth into, so in a sense you have to just plunge into it. It was scary going to South Africa: Timothy West, who played Botha, and I flew out – two English actors to play two South African presidents, there were a lot of South Africans in the film too and I was aware of the irony of the situation and the pressure it carried. But when I made my entrance, made up and in the bald wig, a couple of the extras said 'Ah, Mr President!' so they recognised the visual elements. I had to film a press conference, we actually filmed in the president's palace, and I made the announcement about releasing Mandela. I had to walk out of the palace surrounded by his guards and face about a hundred South African extras playing photographers, and try to convince them that I was the President. I didn't hear any sniggering, which was good. My voice is a bit deeper than his, but I wasn't trying to do an impression. I noted physical elements which helped – when he walked he slightly clenched his fists, and he didn't swing his arms in a relaxed way, they were quite close to his side. They are the sort of details you spot which you can incorporate into a cameo. But I suppose it was the same for Heisenberg, I was aware of a slightly more formal way of holding myself. He was quite formal, but also capable of big physical expression too.

Did Heisenberg's sons see the play in London?

Certainly people who had first-hand experience of him came to see it and I have a vague memory of Frayn and Blakemore showing me a letter, but no one said, 'oh you were a dead ringer for him', but then that is not what we were trying to do.

Copenhagen *provoked huge debate about Heisenberg's role in the Nazi atomic programme. Were you aware when you were performing it of the afterlife it would have?*

To some extent, yes we were, and I have followed the debates since too. The first inkling I had about the interest was Tom Paulin on *The Late Review*, who argued we were trying to exonerate Heisenberg whom he regarded as a war criminal. He was furious. I don't understand how you get that from the play. I think people bring their own baggage and their own interpretation of history, their own sureness of the facts with them. As Frayn explained in his afterword to the play, we do not know whether Heisenberg got the maths wrong or didn't understand it, or deliberately miscalculated. I think some of the criticism is absolutely ludicrous and is based on a complete misunderstanding of the nature of drama. About six major professors have criticised Frayn, but they all criticise him for saying different things, they are all convinced by their own way of seeing that bit of history and they all feel that a piece of drama which posits the possibility of something else is a straight refutation of their beliefs. But I suppose that is what is fascinating about playing real people. I've just finished reading a biography of Mao Tse Tung, and I remember my university mates with their little red books, and now there is evidence to suggest he may have been responsible for the deaths of 70 million of his own people, and that the Cultural Revolution was one of the worst abominations ever. But already there are people saying that that view has gone too far. So history is an ongoing narrative. It is being rewritten all the time. And it is subjective, it is altered by the personal baggage we bring to it.

The controversy and conjecture around the Heisenberg-Bohr meeting enabled David Burke, who played Bohr, to play a practical joke on Michael Frayn. In the play the Nazi scientists were taken to Farm Hall in Cambridgeshire. When we had finished the run at the National and we were rehearsing to go into the West End, David Burke wrote a fake letter to Michael Frayn and Michael Blakemore from a woman called Celia, saying, 'Dear Mr Frayn and Mr Blakemore, I came to see *Copenhagen* because my husband and I honeymooned in Copenhagen, and we saw *Noises Off* which was very funny, so we were hoping for a comedy about the lovely city. Instead, we got a rather boring play about some scientists. But at one point the German chap went on about this place in England, Farm Hall, and we realised it was the place where we had lived for ten years. Whilst we were there we put in central heating, and we dug up the floorboards and found all these letters in German. We threw away lots of them, but we've kept a few – I'll send you one as an example.' David had constructed this elaborate many-paged document, most of which was the German instructions on how to assemble a table tennis table. He'd put a few formulas in, and a drawing of what could be a nuclear reactor, and basically he then indulged in this correspondence with Michael Frayn posing as this fictitious woman Celia. It went on for three months, with David Burke releasing more and more of these false documents, and it sucked Michael in. I was the only person who knew; in fact I was the one that did the dirty on David, and told Michael. The correspondence then continued for another three months with Michael Frayn knowing. The letters have been published in a book called *Celia's Secret or The Copenhagen Papers* (2000). It is fascinating as it also deals with illusion and truth. The two of them tell their side of the story. It is a great read. Of course authentic new documents do sometimes come to light, the Bohr estate have released new documents since we performed the play.

I look back on both *Copenhagen* and *The Jail Diary of Albie Sachs* as extraordinary experiences. But in performance, the controversies and debates don't enter your head. *Copenhagen* is a play, it is not the words of Heisenberg, Bohr or Margrethe. Some plays are different, documentary plays perhaps, where the writer is not trying so much to get into the head of the character as quote from history. If I'd known months in advance I was playing Heisenberg and I'd done an enormous amount of research, and interviewed people, what would I have done if I'd been converted by one of the play's critics? What would have happened if I had become convinced that Heisenberg was a Nazi? My research could have damaged my playing of it. You have to trust the writer. The better the writer, the better the play, the less research you have to do, because it is the playwright's vision of events.

INTERVIEWED BY TOM CANTRELL, LONDON,
25 JUNE 2008

Ian McKellen

Playing D. H. Lawrence, T. E. Lawrence, Adolf Hitler, John Profumo, Tsar Nicholas II and James Whale

Ian McKellen played T. E. Lawrence in *Ross* (1970); D. H. Lawrence in *Priest of Love* (1981); Adolf Hitler in *Countdown to War* (1989); John Profumo in *Scandal* (1989); Tsar Nicholas II in *Rasputin* (1996) and James Whale in *Gods and Monsters* (1998). He also appeared as himself in Ricky Gervais's sitcom, *Extras* (2006).

Perhaps we could start with Gods and Monsters – *how much did you know about James Whale before you played him?*

Nothing. I was starting from scratch. The film is about James Whale, a British film director who had a successful career in Hollywood, notably in 1930s horror films. He directed classics such as *Frankenstein* (1931), *The Invisible Man* (1933) and *The Bride of Frankenstein* (1935). Unusually for Hollywood, he was openly homosexual. The film is very loosely based on a relationship he had with Pierre Foegel, a bartender who became his chauffeur and later his partner. In the film, Foegel's story is changed and he becomes Whale's gardener rather than chauffeur. However, when I started on the project I didn't know any of that.

It so happened I could resemble James Whale by dying my hair white, and we have the same shaped face, but very few people who saw that film knew what Whale looked like. He was just a character in a script by Bill Condon. I did talk to people who knew Whale, and interestingly they all told me something quite different. They spoke of the Whale they knew. You see, we exist in the minds of other people, so our outward appearances are not the sum of who we are. To those who really knew James Whale, I didn't look like him. I looked like Ian McKellen playing James Whale. That is what I am when I am playing anything. I'm fascinated by impersonators, the way they capture elements of a voice without completely capturing it. Yet, I think it is easier to capture aspects of a voice than a face. A face is such a volatile thing. So in focusing on trying to look like the individual, actors are on a hiding to nothing really.

I learnt something early on which is important to playing a real person. I played the soldier T. E. Lawrence ('Lawrence of Arabia') in *Ross*, a television play by Terence Rattigan in 1970, which was based loosely on the facts of his life. During my research I kept finding things out about Lawrence that were not in the play. Since then, I have always told myself that I am not playing a real person, I'm playing a character, who shares a name with a real person. How do you begin to reproduce a real person? Do you write a biography of them? Do you try and look like them? I don't think it helps the audience. Looking like the person seems to me to be not the point of playing a real person. You can never look like them. A similarity may give the audience a kind of frisson, but there would be no point playing any character unless the script is worth doing. In the end, and at the beginning, the actors are at the service of the writer, so you do what is required. If a film like *The Queen* has merits, it has them because of the story being told by Stephen Frears, not the make-up. Acting is not about external things, it is about your inner life.

When I played D. H. Lawrence in the film *Priest of Love* (1981), I went to the place where he and his wife had gone for their honeymoon. There was an old lady there working in the kitchen. who had served them breakfast when they stayed. She saw me and she gasped because she saw a strong resemblance. However, that didn't necessarily make it into a good film. Looking like the person is only a small part of the actor's task and not the most important. You can spend your whole time putting on prosthetics and wigs.

Another example is Hitler in *Countdown to War* (1989). I stuck on the moustache and moved my hair across so I had the same parting as him and I began to look a little bit like him. At least that was my feeling. As for research, you can research to your heart's content, and often you find things that should have gone into the script, but that is the writer's job. My view is that you accept the writer's script or you don't do the production. In *Countdown to War*, all the words I spoke were Hitler's, or reported to have been spoken by him, but of course translation complicates matters further. In terms of impersonating, it is difficult to impersonate a German voice when you are speaking English. I don't think I make much distinction between playing a person a potential audience thinks they know and one whom they don't know. Even if you are playing a real person, the chances are that most people don't know them. It is about the inner life which comes from the script.

Despite what I've said, one distinction between playing a real person and a fictional character is that you can be precise about physicality. I'm an actor who likes to discover the character partly through physicality. If you have a photograph or film footage, you can copy it or you note things and apply them to yourself. That can help in my process and make me confident that I can impersonate the character. All acting is impersonating in a sense. Usually the clues are only in the script but you do have a few more clues if you are playing a real person. Although reading biographies and talking to their friends is, in my experience, not necessarily very helpful.

Early on, I find it very useful to get acquainted with the physicality of the person: their appearance, the sound of their voice, their vocal characteristics, the way they walk, the way they hold themselves, the way they sit. You only need to get one characteristic right, one gesture which you have observed, and you can use your actor's imagination and apply it to the rest of your body and to their mind. Therefore, when playing a real person, you can get a bit ahead of the game. Most scripts don't describe in detail how a character walks or talks or looks, so if the person you are playing is a good model, that can really help. For example, when I looked at films of Hitler, I discovered that he had something wrong with his spine, which was a very useful thing to know. He was constantly straining against it in the way he walks and so that is conveyed through the body and into the personality. He was short. Obviously I'm a lot taller than he was, so I wouldn't try to make myself small, I would try to imagine the psychology behind a man who wants to be taller. He makes up for it in other ways. I was not copying the external things, but working out how they affect the internal mechanisms.

In Countdown to War, *the focus is on Hitler in private and at work, not in public. As a lot of the footage of Hitler is of his public side, how did you approach playing the private man?*

Again it was about the way in which external features affected the internal. I closely observed the way he walked and the way he liked to show off and present himself. His outer confidence was against all the odds, because he wasn't a pretty fellow. He wasn't handsome, his body was a bit of a wreck and I thought those facts helped. He had to give a lot of energy to resist giving in to his bad back. He was constantly uncomfortable in his body. He liked to show off but he knew that what he had to show off wasn't attractive. It was interesting that in *Countdown to War* there were so many of us playing real people that I think in the end we found it rather inhibiting actually. We felt we were going to stand or fall by whether we were credible as the people we were playing.

Playing a real person can give you all sorts of little insights that perhaps the writer has taken for granted, but the danger is that you find something you want to incorporate into a part which the writer has not. For example, when I played T. E. Lawrence in *Ross*, it seemed to me that his sexuality was a big problem for him. Like many adventurers who left England, what he was escaping from was his sexuality. He found some sort of satisfaction in the East, but making that too explicit in the script wasn't practical because the writer wasn't interested in that particular angle. In fact, I remember I read biographies that had been written after the script, so I knew more about him than the writer. You are playing the playwright's version of the person.

Clearly, there is a big difference between my experiences and a film like *The Queen*. If that film hadn't convinced you that Helen Mirren looked like the Queen, then the thrill of seeing her would be a lot less. But I have met the Queen and if you've been up close to her, she is nothing like Helen Mirren, she is tiny. That is the remarkable thing about the Queen – she is amazingly small. But does the physical difference matter? I saw Prunella Scales play the Queen in *A Question of Attribution* (1982) by Alan Bennett. When Prunella first entered as the Queen it crossed my mind, 'has the Queen nothing better to do?!' She was incredibly convincing. When she came on at the end and did a curtain call, it was extremely unsettling as the Queen does not bow to anyone. I've never really played anyone with such significant current celebrity.

You say you haven't played anyone like that, but John Profumo was quite recognisable.

That's true. Profumo was a Conservative politician who became part of a huge media scandal in 1963 when he had a brief relationship with showgirl, Christine Keeler, who (at the height of Cold War tensions) was reputedly also a mistress of a Russian spy. The film, *Scandal*, premiered in 1989. I was dreadful as Profumo. I had a very unfortunate haircut, trying to copy his receding hair, which taught me subsequently always to look into the mirror from the side. I was rewarded with a series of reviews that only mentioned my haircut. I would have done much better not trying to look like him at all. To know what school he went to would probably tell you more about him than any photograph. So I found that very tricky and unsatisfactory, but it wasn't really a leading part. The script wasn't delving into how this man came to be the way he is, the script was more about Stephen Ward, an acquaintance of Profumo who introduced him to Keeler at a party. Ward was charged with living off the profits of prostitution, but committed suicide on the last day of his trial. He was played by John Hurt who did a fantastic job, though whether he looked anything like Stephen Ward I don't know.

Did it make any difference to you that he was still alive when you played him?

Oh yes, I wrote to him and said I'd been asked to play him in a film and before accepting I wanted to give him the opportunity to express a view, but he didn't reply.

You never heard anything from him?

No. A couple of his friends protested against the film, saying it was quite inappropriate to drag up these events, but I disagreed. I thought they were important things to be reminded of about people in public life. I think everyone else I have played was dead. So Profumo was an exception. Interestingly, I didn't think I played him very well. If it had been a leading character I might have been more at ease with it, but all the time I tried to be like someone I wasn't. Acting is about delving into your own experiences and putting elements of yourself at the disposal of the character. It is always yourself and you imagine yourself into another situation. The make up and the look-a-like aspect is titillating but it is not the essence.

Do you think you can ever get the essence of somebody through observation? Or would it be purely from the script?

You learn from looking at pictures of yourself that photographs are very unreliable, as are film clips. You'd have to meet the person, and then all sorts of things are revealed to you, which you would then explore for yourself. So if I was playing someone who was desperately nervous and had tics of one sort or another, the point for me wouldn't be to copy their tics immaculately, but to note that he is the sort of person who has to be constantly doing something with his hands. I'd probably invent my own mannerisms. The observation wouldn't therefore be based on what he looks like when he is nervous, but rather on the fact he is nervous.

Did your view of Profumo change through playing him?

Not really, no, because the script wasn't revealing. Even with James Whale, who was a leading character, the film was based on a fictionalised version of his life. You have to ask how much you can say in a 90-minute movie.

One major difference with playing a real person is the responsibility you feel towards the individual. You want to do the right thing by them. That is why I wrote to Profumo. But the family of James Whale who saw *Gods and Monsters*, the people who knew him best, didn't like it. Profumo's friends didn't want the film to be made. I don't know what the Queen thought. I suppose her advisors told her that she'd come out of it very well, that it was rather good PR. Frears said that his two main characters, the Queen and Tony Blair, were both passive in the events depicted, so to make the film he had to make Tony Blair very pro-active and so gave him words he would probably never say. What is the point, then, of looking like the character whilst saying things he never said? It is all fiction. Richard III is the same, he was not deformed in the way that Shakespeare invented. So is there any point in reading histories about him?

Did you feel a pressure to meet public expectations of what these historical figures should be like?

Yes, because that is part of the reason the film is being made – to give people that little bit of thrill that they are getting close to an iconic or famous person whom they will never have a chance of meeting. When I played Tsar Nicholas II in *Rasputin* (1996), I was in a cathedral in Leningrad and there were some old people there who crossed themselves as I went by. That was very gratifying but I was six inches taller and, in my view, didn't look that much like him.

The willingness of the audience to project onto you what they want to see is intriguing.

Yes, they don't know the person. As I have said, the people who did know the individuals I played found the impersonation quite unsatisfactory. It is an impossible thing to do. The amazing thing about the human race is that, with the exception of identical twins and triplets, we are all different. We go into certain groupings, you see faces that are similar, but you've never seen that particular face before. So to try and impersonate someone, when we are so different, is impossible. But when playing a real person I might just be kick-started by seeing a picture or a bit of film footage.

Were there any other physicalities that were helpful?

Well, I could tell from the way James Whale stood and the cut of the clothes he liked wearing that he was a bit of a dandy. I saw a nude painting that he'd done of an Aryan beauty, which I think was an idealised portrait of himself. I thought it was interesting that that was how he wanted to be, and yet he was a handsome man. He posed quite a bit for photographs. I'm not saying he posed all day long, but he was a film director, so naturally interested in what the camera caught. That doesn't mean to say I copied his poses, but I noted that he was the sort of man who might pose. I don't suppose that was actually mentioned in the script, so that is an example of where a little bit of research helped.

One of Whale's friends, the director Curtis Harrington, appeared in a cameo role in the film. Did you have conversations with him?

It was a relief when he gave me the thumbs up, but Whale had been dead for 40 years. So what was the old Curtis Harrington remembering? Memory works in strange ways. We see someone like Elena Roger's performance as *Piaf* or Jane Lapotaire in the original production, and we say it is like being there, like seeing them in the flesh. Piaf was tiny, and completely different from both actresses, but I suppose these iconic people have certain characteristics to which we respond. If the impersonator, as opposed to the actor, lands on enough of those points, such as the quaver in the voice, or a particular stance or gesture, then audiences are willing to suspend disbelief. I saw Jim Bailey play Judy Garland and it was fantastic! It was an impression. He is a man, but with lighting effects and by capturing elements of the voice, he got enough of her famous characteristics to give an impression.

Would you describe the work you have done as an 'impression'?

Well, I'm not talented as an impersonator and I don't view my work in that way really. Impersonation is entertaining, but acting is something deeper than that. It is not just about appearances, it is about the inner life. Now as an actor I like dressing up, I like disguise. I like not looking like the same person.

Do you think there are different demands between theatre and screen work in terms of playing a real person?

In a film if you put someone in a wig that resembles the Queen's hair, and don't show her full length, have her sitting down, and copy the voice, that is enough. Put the Queen next to Helen Mirren dressed as the Queen, there is not a person in the world who would confuse them. It is all an illusion created by the costume and the camera. In the theatre you see the whole body all the time. You can look at it. An editor hasn't got in the way. You can't direct the audience's gaze like you can in a film. With impersonation, the way the camera takes a shot of you, and the way you are lit is going to be very crucial and very precise in a way it couldn't be in a theatre. That is why Prunella Scales's performance of the Queen was so remarkable – she was utterly convincing. The Queen walks very slowly. That is the first thing that occurs to you when you see her. She walks very slowly so you get a chance to look at her. She is a woman who is aware she is being looked at. That is the first thing you are aware of, people staring at her. You can detect she doesn't like it. Now that characteristic is what you would hold onto if you were playing the part. Whether you look like her or not doesn't matter – it is not as interesting as that character note.

Another person you have played is yourself in Ricky Gervais's sitcom, Extras.

Now that was unnerving.

Why was that?

It was scary how I could land on those bits of myself that were all too appropriate for this pompous idiot. I have seen interviews with myself subsequently in which I seem to be playing that again! I have had to amend in myself the way I act in interview. I try now not to present myself too much. It is something you cannot get away from; we all do it. Our behaviour is all about presenting ourselves. I hate being photographed as myself – I don't know how to present myself because I don't know what I am. Whenever I see what I do when I arrange myself, I see this idiot. So that was very instructive! In an interview you select bits of yourself to present. You are not being yourself. You are being a version of yourself. That is acting, and when you realise that the acting of yourself is a character you don't really like, it is unnerving.

Performing is a very human activity. As Shakespeare said, 'All the world's a stage and all the men and women merely players.' He was fascinated by the fact that we are all acting all day long, that we wear costumes, they are not just clothes. If we just wanted to keep warm we wouldn't care about the colour or the style, but people go to great lengths to choose which socks to wear. They wear different socks for different situations. If you are going to work, the minute you wake up you decide what to wear, what is appropriate. You decide whether or not to show off. We easily modify our language, our vocabulary, our attitude according to the company we are keeping. That is what human beings do. We have refined our performances to a huge extent. We send out signals that are almost invisible but they are there. A lot of it is conscious, and some unconscious, but all of it, you would have to say, is acting. Humans are not the same all day long. It can be unnerving if you are with your mother and you meet your girlfriend, suddenly you don't know which part to play. You feel uncomfortable. So acting is a very human activity and I think that is why some people are interested in acting as a process – hence your book.

INTERVIEWED BY TOM CANTRELL, NEWCASTLE,
24 APRIL 2009

David Morrissey

Playing Gordon Brown

David Morrissey played Gordon Brown in *The Deal* (Channel 4, 2003), directed by Stephen Frears and scripted by Peter Morgan. He won a Royal Television Society Award for Best Actor for his performance and the drama won the British Academy Award for Best Single Drama.

How did you come to be cast as Gordon Brown?

I'd played a fictional MP called Stephen Collins in *State of Play*, a political drama written by Paul Abbott and broadcast by the BBC in 2003. My research had involved meeting a lot of politicians and shadowing Peter Mandelson. I wanted to get the details of a politician's job right, especially for an MP whose constituency was outside London. I was struck by the volume of time they spend in meetings, commuting and travelling from one place to another. I was fascinated by the machine of politics, the ambition and adrenalin, and the clubbable atmosphere of the political parties and of Westminster. One day I bumped into the producer for *The Deal* and she asked me to audition for the role. I was quite surprised by the suggestion.

Why?

Firstly, I thought it was intriguing that a drama was being written about a current politician, a man very much in the news and not a historical figure. Secondly, I didn't regard myself as an obvious casting choice. I don't look or sound like Gordon Brown in any way. He was born in 1951 and I'm a fair bit younger. I read the script and found it compelling. I also read James Naughties's book *The Rivals: The Intimate Portrait of a Political Marriage* (2002), about the relationship between Gordon Brown and Tony Blair, which covered the same ground as the film. *The Deal* depicts the friendship between Brown and Blair from 1983 when both are first elected to Parliament, through to 1997, when Blair became Prime Minister and Brown became Chancellor of the Exchequer in the New Labour government. Even in 2003 Gordon Brown was still a rather mysterious figure, eclipsed by Blair but perceived as the much greater intellect, and the man whose economic prowess kept Blair in power. I thought the film was very topical because there were all sorts of rumours about the stresses between them: the film studies the tensions in their relationship, the creativity of their partnership, but also the dark battle of personal and political ambition between them. It culminates in the well-documented pact allegedly made in the Granita restaurant in London, when Brown took the decision not to stand in the 1994 Labour leadership election so that Blair could become the uncontested leader of the Party, and later Prime Minister. It's a cleverly crafted piece of writing because you ask how different history might have been had Brown not stood aside.

Did you do research for the audition?

Stephen Frears is admirable in that, unlike many directors, he won't enter into a project before the whole cast is in place. The audition was tough – he really needed me to convince him that I could do it. I did a little research preparation for the audition, recording Brown on the TV so that I could analyse his speech patterns and begin to work out how he talked. I also organised a couple of sessions with my voice coach and we worked on the features of his voice. In the audition Stephen saw that the role was reachable for me. I got the part and went off to do serious research and work.

How did you prepare for the role?

I tried to set up a meeting with Gordon Brown, but that was never going to happen! I always find it very important to work out exactly where your character comes from, especially if they are real people. Who are his parents? What did they do? Who were his grandparents? Where did he grow up and what was happening in his formative years? I read a book by Paul Routledge, *Gordon Brown: The Biography* (1998). I also watched two documentaries about the Labour Party by Ross Wilson: one covered the six months leading up to the general election in 1994 and the other covered the six months following the 1994 general election. The interesting thing about those documentaries was that Gordon Brown was shown not just publicly, speaking at the dispatch box and at various meetings and public events, but also privately and because he knew Ross Wilson he was more relaxed than you might expect.

I met up with a lot of people who knew him publicly and privately, both politicians and political commentators, and built up a picture of him. I made extensive notes and wrote out what I thought were the most important incidents from Paul Routledge's book as they related to the script. A lot of the research you can't use because it might not be relevant to the script, but I find very significant insights working in this way. I watched endless footage; that's the fortunate thing about playing a current, high-profile politician – there was no lack of material. If I'd been playing Lord Byron I'd have been looking at portraits and art works. The material for research is much more prolific for a famous contemporary figure. I could note, for example, how Brown sits, walks and how he fiddles with his papers when he's speaking. But the availability of the material doesn't necessarily make it easier as an actor because the political sensitivity of the drama was complicated and the script came via a lawyer for much of the time.

Did you go to Brown's constituency?

I walked around Kirkcaldy, where he grew up and his constituency since 1983 when he was elected to Parliament. I looked at the church and the schools he'd attended and the local haunts. When you play a real person you don't want to take anything for granted – if information or an environment is there and it's tangible, I try to seek it out. There are things you can only learn for yourself: for example, Kirkcaldy used to have a large linoleum factory when Brown was growing up and the stink from it pervaded the whole town. Whilst the people are friendly, the environment is dull, dark, and it's often throwing it down with rain. It's a harsh place and there can be a cutting wind. You've got to be tough to survive that environment and the sheer battle against the elements gives you ideas about posture.

Brown's father was a minister of the Church of Scotland and his mother was the daughter of a timber merchant. He was one of three sons and came from a family with strong morals and a father who was known for his ability to give great sermons. He idolised his parents. He had already established a reputation for himself by the age of 16 when he became the youngest post-war student at Edinburgh University. He'd blazed a path at school where there was a system to fast-track the brightest pupils and he'd jumped up two years. It was a system he later critiqued because he saw the emotional price that some of his friends paid who didn't have the resources to deal with the pressure – but he could take it. His teachers said that they could never give him enough work.

There was an event at school which was particularly interesting for me as an actor. Just before he went to university he played in a school rugby match and was knocked unconscious. Both retinas in his eyes detached and he lost the sight in one eye; the sight in the other was saved by pioneering surgery. He endured painful surgery and months of recuperation when he had to lie in a darkened room. At a time when he should have been socialising, meeting women, and enjoying a little independence he was struck down. His life was on hold and there was the danger of total blindness. That's got to have a profound effect on anyone and for me it explained why Brown has always been a man in a hurry. His energy and commitment are colossal and he has all the adrenalin to go with that: he fidgets constantly and he's a terrible nail-biter. All these things are interesting to play.

You have a range of facial expressions for Brown, including a particularly dark frown. How did you work on those?

My expressions come from what my character is thinking. I inhabit the character. I don't adopt a look for the sake of it – that's what impersonation is. You have to be careful about that when you're acting a real person in a serious drama. Because of the eye problem Brown can come across as rather remote and his mouth is slightly skewed when he speaks, but it's dangerous to become too idiosyncratic. You mustn't go overboard.

When I spoke to friends of his, they informed me that he is very funny – which I found astonishing. Women who'd met him told me that he is tremendously sexy and a man of great passion.

How did you understand the process of playing Gordon Brown?

I wasn't doing an impersonation or an imitation. In fact I spoke to Rory Bremner whose impersonations are brilliant, of course. Rory has finessed the comic sketch and is concerned with characters whom he plays for short periods; playing a character for a full-length drama is not the same. The comic sketch and the drama involve different acting disciplines. For me, it was important to get to a place where I could know Gordon Brown the man and be surprised by what I knew.

ITV dropped the drama because of worries about its political sensitivity and Channel 4 took it on. Did you have any political anxieties?

Yes, I did. Blair and Brown were running the country and you cannot afford to get facts or details wrong. Lawyers worried about libel and possible kickback. My wife tells the story of the night I woke in a panic at 3am, saying, 'I can't do this! I can't do this!' I felt I was being disloyal to someone I admired. I also worried that my efforts to play him could only be ridiculed – which is common actor paranoia. However, the story needed telling and the media and public reception certainly proved that.

What was the most charged scene for you as an actor? The press all wrote about the scene in the Granita restaurant.

Yes, I know, but for me the most charged scene was the funeral of the Labour leader, John Smith in 1994, who died so suddenly. At the moment when Brown should have been at his most galvanised and organising his leadership campaign, he lost his great friend and political mentor and was overtaken by grief. Fatally, Brown felt that the leadership was his by right and that he wouldn't experience any serious challenge to it. While Brown was dealing with the death of his friend, Tony Blair's camp took the reins and made a charge for power. Brown had always refused to run against Smith because he felt he owed his career to him. By the time he'd woken up to what was happening he'd lost the campaign to Blair. It's the explosively unpredictable concoction of politics and personality. Brown is very straight with people, some would say to the point of rudeness (I've heard stories of Brown screaming in the corridors of Downing Street – which isn't going to win you any friends); Blair was the pacifier, charmer and manipulator. But when Brown expected loyalty and support from his friends, they'd been won over by Blair. Is that opportunism or treachery? It's the nature of politics. It's absolutely fascinating how personality and emotion can dictate history.

How important was the chemistry between you and Michael Sheen, who played Tony Blair?

Extremely important. He's a great actor and a friend of mine. The trust between us as actors was essential. We would always work on our scenes together before shooting.

Were you surprised by the enormous buzz that the film created?

When you're actually doing the work you have very little idea of how it will turn out. Michael Sheen and I were worried that our representations of these two major politicians would be universally derided. I saw the first screening with Stephen Frears and felt that we had definitely realised the quality of Peter Morgan's script, but I was still worried about the film's reception. The next screening I attended was at Channel 4 with all the journalists present. I'm used to dealing with the entertainment and arts journalists and know many of them well, but when I looked round the room I realised it was crammed with all the political journalists. I saw Andrew Marr and Michael White and panicked. Michael White ran out of the room and I thought, oh god, he hated it! – But then he ran back and said that he couldn't stay but that he'd found it riveting. What the film portrayed is that the relationship between these two men has, at certain times, been a great help to our country and, at others, been a terrible hindrance because their bureaucratic games with one another sometimes consumed them more than their duties as politicians. The film also highlighted that the difficulties New Labour ran into were evident at the very beginning and epitomised in the relationship between Brown and Blair and their different political styles. There was a real frisson in the room and a realisation that the drama had exposed and articulated something that political journalists had been expressing for years. It was very exciting and proof that drama can generate important political debate.

Do you have any final points to make about playing Gordon Brown?

You don't create a role on your own. Peter Morgan's script was fantastic. My voice coach was invaluable. I had hairdressers and make-up artists working on my hair and my face to create a resemblance to Gordon Brown – a great deal of labour went into that. I could choose the exact brown of the contact lenses I wanted to wear. I think we got the essence of him.

I was very impressed by the sheer amount of research that was done for *The Deal* – during the shooting and editing stages as well. When I asked for material I was sent a vast amount and loved that commitment. When you're playing a living person who is constantly in the public eye and in such a significant position you have to research the political situation all the time. You have to respond to information that is coming in because the situation changes constantly. If information comes in repeatedly which contradicts what's in the script, you *have* to deal with it. Peter Morgan was always alert to that, as were the producers, and there were constant discussions about accuracy. I've watched some political dramas since and thought they were too intent on taking a swipe at the political protagonists. You can't take liberties like that in my view. You must keep an eye on the information flow as an actor playing a real person. Like a journalist, you have to be able to corroborate your decisions with facts, not hearsay. You can't play fast and loose with the public.

Have you met Gordon Brown subsequently?

I have and he didn't mention anything about the film. I suspect he hasn't seen it!

TELEPHONE INTERVIEW BY MARY LUCKHURST,
23 JANUARY 2009

Joseph Mydell

Playing Robert Mugabe

Joseph Mydell appeared as the President of Zimbabwe, Robert Mugabe, in Fraser Grace's play, *Breakfast with Mugabe*, directed by Antony Sher and produced by the Royal Shakespeare Company, in 2005.

How did you first become acquainted with the part?

In 2003 there was a read-through with the Royal Shakespeare Company in London. At that time the play had about 12 characters and the focus was rather different. Fraser was trying to show the suffering and deprivation in the small villages of Zimbabwe and how Mugabe's regime was affecting them. The most interesting scenes focused on Mugabe and his white, settler psychiatrist and the other scenes simply seemed to be obstructing what was a potentially riveting confrontation. At a later date Antony Sher took on the play and asked Fraser to focus on the *ngozi*, the ghost that haunts Mugabe, and the relationship between the President and his psychiatrist. By 2005 the script had been substantially re-worked and Tony Sher asked me to come and read for the part. I was really delighted that he wanted me to do it.

How did you begin to work on the part in rehearsals?

We had about four weeks of rehearsal and began with a few days of intensive improvisation. A musician, Chartwell Dutiro, played Zimbabwean music which I found plaintive and unearthly, and we did improvisations around the theme of Mugabe's vulnerability and his extreme suspicion of others. There was one scenario where I was blindfolded and the other actors mocked me, led me, tricked me and shouted at me. It had an extraordinarily powerful effect on me. I experienced deep visceral fear and paranoia, both of these, of course, were important for the role. Mugabe doesn't trust anyone and the improvisations explored his need for complete control. He doesn't trust his wife who is much younger and a ruthless consumer of Western goods; he cannot trust his political colleagues nor his military men. He ensures obedience through brutal suppression. He does not trust the psychiatrist because of a pathological hatred of whites whom he sees as colonial leaches. I remember another improvisation of a moment in the play when Mrs Mugabe is describing how her husband places a bowl of food on the dinner table for the *ngozi*, the spirit who is haunting and terrifying him. An *ngozi* is a malevolent, vengeful spirit who must be appeased or the subject will be pursued to their grave. It's reminiscent of the scene where Macbeth sees Banquo's ghost but the rest of the party see nothing. The object of the exercise was to put fear and terror into the heart of Mrs Mugabe and other observers.

All through this we had an assistant director who helped us with all the background material. I read the first biography on Mugabe, which was printed in the 1980s and recounted how he'd risen to prominence as a Zimbabwe African National Union leader in the guerrilla war against white-minority rule in Rhodesia in the Bush War from 1964–79. Like Mandela he went to prison for his championing of resistance. In the 1980s Mugabe was hailed as a hero: he served as Prime Minister from 1980–87 and has been Zimbabwe's President since 1987, both constitutionally and now unconstitutionally. It's difficult to believe, but he was not then the tyrant he is today: after decades of brutal, white colonial rule and civil war he represented a victory against apartheid. He was the delight and hope of everybody in the West.

Did you read other biographies?

Yes, two of them were: Martin Meredith's *Our Votes, Our Guns: Robert Mugabe and the Tragedy of Zimbabwe* (2002) and *Robert Mugabe and the Betrayal of Zimbabwe* (2003) by Andrew Norman. I watched clips of him as well. After a few days Tony told me that I needed to find Mugabe's physicality and lose my own amiable self, what he referred to as 'Uncle Joe'. From then on it was agreed that I would dress formally in a jacket and tie for every rehearsal. It created an instant authority. I began to experiment with jutting my head forward, and making my shoulders more rounded and one day I walked in and Tony said 'That's it!' I observed the way Mugabe moved – wanting to appear youthful and all-powerful. I likened myself to a tank powering over everything in my path, my eyes were the double gun barrels focusing on anybody in the way and ready to destroy them, particularly the psychiatrist if he got out of hand. That's how the character developed.

Did you use film footage a lot in your preparation?

I did, particularly for his speech patterns. We had a vocal coach who was wonderful and wrote out everything phonetically for us. I worked on his speech pattern, his accent, his gait, the walk, the physicality, but also on his emotional base for the play. He's utterly terrified because of the ghost that only he can see, but is enraged when the psychiatrist gets too close to the psychological truth. I had to go into very dark places in myself. The feeling of absolute power over the fate of others was simultaneously exhilarating and frightening. The more I felt that power, the more I embraced it, the better the performance. It was non-negotiable. But it was a complex business of construction too: I had to operate on all these cylinders, all the time, and it was very exhausting. Mugabe is highly intelligent, which is the tragedy of it: he has seven degrees, he was raised by Jesuits and began life as a teacher, as someone who valued education and learning but is ending his life by destroying a country and its peoples. How do you reconcile all the contradictions in this man? The play does have a Shakespearean quality in the sense that Mugabe was a great man who has sunk into tyranny, violence and corruption, like Macbeth. On the first night I made my entrance, which had terrific impact, I moved in, bullet-like, towards David Rintoul, the psychiatrist, but addressed the bodyguard, not him. As I walked out I heard a gasp from the audience and I learned afterwards that some Zimbabweans had thought I was uncannily like Mugabe himself: I worked on every detail from the film footage, the way he stands, moves, holds his hands, juts his head. There's a section when the psychiatrist has the upper hand and is really pushing Mugabe, questioning him about a former colleague and political rival who was killed under mysterious circumstances. The suggestion is that Mugabe may have had him executed. When the psychiatrist suggests that Mugabe had a homosexual minister arrested, I exploded internally. Mugabe is wildly homophobic. I crossed the stage and pointed at the psychiatrist in the way I had observed Mugabe point – a gesture that means 'you're done for'. You use such gestures strategically and with absolute economy – Tony was very rigorous about that.

How else did Tony Sher enable you to find the character of Mugabe?

Of course, Tony has played all these great monsters and so I asked him how do you play a dictator, a violent fiend? He was fascinating because he was interested in what makes them human so he focused me on Mugabe's vulnerability and the rawness of his emotions. The key moment was the revelation about the child, the son from whom Mugabe was forcibly removed when he was imprisoned. The son died of encephalitis and Ian Smith, the Prime Minister of Rhodesia at the time, refused to allow him to attend the funeral. It was an extraordinary lack of mercy and burial is extremely important in African tradition. Fraser embedded this as a major revelation in the play and as a key to his character. He could never forgive. It was a deep-rooted rage, a bitter horror and grief. A personal tragedy made political. I had to stop myself from crying and Tony emphasised that it was important always to have the tears there, but to hold them back. Understanding these emotional roots for playing Mugabe was critical because what I see and what the public sees is the monster now, the dictator who won't resign. The play explores what lies behind that and the death of his young son became an important anchor for me. In contrast to that vulnerability is the extremity of his need for control and power, his obsession with the display of power, his explosive unpredictability, ruthlessness and violence. His vulnerability made him real to me.

Did your preparation for this play differ from when you work on an invented character?

I'm stating the obvious but there are sources outside oneself with a real character, though the physical construction of a character is immensely creative. I love the work of the actor: you create, but you are creating from material that has been provided and then you shape that material. The play is like a rock and the actor sculpts away, trying to find out what is in this huge rock. Rodin once said that he never knew how his sculptures were going to turn out because he had to see what was in the stone. That's how I feel about acting. There is probably only one rule of thumb I have as an actor, which is that I always look at where the character ends up, and then I work my way backwards to figure out how he gets to that point. How can Mugabe end up exuding all this power? Where does he get all that from? So I examined everything earlier on to find out. You have to know every sinew and the muscle of the character. With Tony Sher I created this monster onstage. He was alive, and, yes, he was real, for those 123 minutes, this was our creation and it was substantiated by all the things we discussed, explored and researched. At the end, Mugabe's power is mirrored by his merciless reduction of the psychiatrist to helpless victim, whose wife has been murdered, whose farm workers have been attacked, and whose land is in jeopardy. The psychiatrist pays for his naïvety, for his belief that he can influence Mugabe and protect his property, but most of all for his belief that he has an inalienable right to his farmland – the land that his ancestors stole from black Africans.

So when you say that an actor creates from a blank canvas, or block of stone, is it stressful to play a real person who has already been constructed in the public perception?

It was a great sense of responsibility. In this play, unlike other obvious examples that deal with dictators, the protagonist is not written as a caricature. With Alfred Jarry's *Ubu Roi* or Brecht's *Arturo Ui*, the extremity of the construction dictates a certain performance style. But *Breakfast with Mugabe* is like a chamber piece, confined to one room, and Mugabe is both pursued and pursuing. This is a play that operates behind the scenes and examines how Mugabe functions off camera. The speech at the rally was not originally in the play and Tony Sher argued that it needed to be written. It's a crucial scene because it is the public performance of power, his performance as a politician, the master tyrant. Fraser sets up an image wonderfully and then undercuts it. I could taste the words in the rally speech, I could really enjoy the cruelty of it, and the defiance of the West.

Tony's direction was vital to my performance. It was his directorial debut, so we had him at a heightened state of creativity as he was doing something for the first time; he was giving us everything he understood about psychology and physical characterisation, about theatre, about timing, pace and line learning. At one point I got extremely angry at Tony and I didn't know whether it was as the character or as myself. I said, 'Oh sometimes I get so angry with you', and he said, 'Oh really Joe? As Mugabe or you?', and I said, 'What difference does it make!', because I was so frustrated by that time with the character. It happened at the point when all the elements of physicality, emotion, accent, gesture were coming together and one element might easily slip and I'd feel unbelievably aggravated. When the character did come together I was elated. I had to be so alert. When you play a character that the public knows you have to take them to places that the public doesn't know, otherwise you're indulging in caricature or you're doing an impersonation like Rory Bremner, and no matter how good that might be, it is not what sustains a play. I never thought I was impersonating him, and I was very careful after the show each night to cut off from the character psychologically and I'd always make sure that I dressed as differently as possible from Mugabe. There was one night I was at the bus stop and two girls approached me, and asked me if I'd met Mugabe. One said: 'You are like him, just like him, the way you move your hand and everything it is just like him.' You have to remember that Mugabe was born in 1924 and I am significantly younger. She continued. 'You know there is a reference to Grace Mugabe's niece, well I am one of the nieces and I'm going to tell my family they must come and see you.' And I thought oh Jesus! Oh god I've had it now, I'm going to get blown off the stage! Clearly, I had captured certain external qualities. Mugabe's 'men' did come to see the show, in their dark suits, and they took notes but they gave a thumbs up to the musician so I think they liked it! I was as conscious of Mugabe's detractors as I was his supporters while I was playing the part. There were protests opposing his regime while the play was on and I went and gave the protestors publicity about the play. That really added a tension to doing this part. I had a slight apprehension about whether Mugabe would hear about my activities and what might happen. The play is about a character, but as an actor I had to be able to argue precisely, factually, intellectually what he had done prior to becoming this appalling man. I knew those biographies very well.

Was that before rehearsals?

Yes. I knew so much about him. I had to because it's necessary to understand as much as you can. I had to know what informed Fraser's argument. In my working process as an actor I always do a lot of research. I want to know what informs what the character is saying, and if it is something I have to invent, I invent it. I don't tell anyone necessarily. I may have some discussion with the director but in the end there are certain things you keep to yourself as an actor. As a character, he controls everyone on stage, the whole environment. That first exchange, when Mugabe coerces the psychiatrist into accepting a tie that he doesn't want, is a brilliant piece of writing. The psychiatrist's fate is already sealed but the audience doesn't know it. It's a microcosm of the entire play, like a piece of music and you see variations on it.

Did you have any apprehension about playing Mugabe?

It was an extraordinary challenge to play someone so unthinkably powerful in the modern world, to try and find out what made him tick. I read about other dictators like Haile Selassie, Mobutu in Zaire, Lumumba from the Congo, but what distinguishes Mugabe from other African dictators is that he is a strategist, an intellectual and not a military man. I found that very interesting. He's hung onto power because he was their intellectual superior. But it's also his tragedy – he's now a die-hard, Zimbabwe is in economic ruin and poverty, political corruption and suffering are rife. He seems to have had no plan. He's far more preoccupied with maintaining power at any cost than he is with governing a country, solving its problems and caring for its population. What a tragedy that he does not seek to meliorate the conditions of this tragic country. And I made no excuses for that when I played him. More than anything else I wanted to show how power corrupts and what the consequences are of misusing power.

It sounds as though playing Mugabe had a very powerful impact on your psyche.

I'd say that the playing Mugabe ended up being a kind of possession. It's very interesting because the character is convinced he is being haunted, and I felt I was being possessed by this man, this monster. And at the same time, I was seeing a therapist about events earlier in my life, and about the arrival of my 17-year-old daughter on my doorstep who wanted to live with me. I don't think I would have had the emotional strength to do this part if I hadn't myself been able to talk about things that were unresolved from my own past. It was an extraordinary time for me, very special, and all of that added to the creation of this role.

INTERVIEWED BY TOM CANTRELL, LONDON,
11 NOVEMBER 2007

Michael Pennington

*Playing Wilhelm Furtwängler, Richard Strauss,
King George III, Charles Dickens, Robert Maxwell
and Anton Chekhov*

Michael Pennington played conductor and composer Wilhelm Furtwängler (1886–1954) in *Taking Sides* and composer Richard Strauss (1864–1949) in *Collaboration*, both by Ronald Harwood (Minerva Theatre, Chichester, 2008 and Duchess Theatre, London, 2009); George III in Alan Bennett's *The Madness of George III* (West Yorkshire Playhouse, 2003); Charles Dickens in Simon Gray's *Little Nell* (Theatre Royal, Bath, 2007); Robert Maxwell in Ian Curteis's *The Bargain* (National Tour, 2007); and Anton Chekhov in *A Wife Like the Moon* (TV, 1982) and in a one-man show, *Anton Chekhov* (1984).

You played the American soldier, Major Steve Arnold in the premiere of Taking Sides *in 1995 directed by Harold Pinter, and now, in 2008, you're playing the German composer Furtwängler. So you're performing in the play for a second time, playing a different character.*

It's been as interesting as you would imagine. When I was first asked to do it again I was concerned that, in a metaphorical sense, I wouldn't get the music of the first production out of my head because we did it for a long time – maybe 200 performances. Obviously I remember Daniel Massey's remarkable performance as Furtwängler, but it was surprising how quickly that all vanished when we started working on the play. It was very much like the experience of returning to a classic play by Chekhov or by Shakespeare, which takes endless revisiting and reinterpretation. I think *Taking Sides* is a modern classic. It can be reinterpreted every time; there are passages and lines in it that reverberate today even more than they did in 1995.

Can you give an example?

Yes, there's certainly a potency in one of Furtwängler's final lines to Major Arnold when he turns round to him at the end of the play and says, 'Major, what kind of a world do you want? What kind of world are you going to make?' It was always a powerful line, spoken by a German aesthete to an American soldier in 1946 but, without forcing the point, in 2008 for any European to say these words to any American has a particular resonance. But this production also takes a different shape and is in many ways different from its predecessor.

How do you begin to approach playing an historical figure?

Of course, both central characters in *Taking Sides* are fictional to the extent that Furtwängler is a writer's portrait of a real person: part of the dramatist's job has been to underline certain elements of his character and to play down others for the purposes of the drama. Equally, Steve Arnold is, in a way, based on a real man – the American interrogators of suspected Nazi sympathisers in Berlin in 1946 were often from the Mid-West, from Milwaukee for instance, because they tended to be German-speaking and were able to conduct the interviews more successfully. So although he's a fictional creation, he's based on the kind of American who *might* have been one of this rather shadowy group in Berlin in 1946 who were really out to get Furtwängler – in a way that the Russians and British were not. Nobody quite knows who they were because nothing was minuted but it seems likely that there was such a group, who were ferocious about wanting to nail Furtwängler as a Nazi collaborator. Steve Arnold is based not so much on a real character as on a real model.

Did you research what you could about the interrogations when you played Major Arnold in the premiere?

Yes, I did. I was in America and I went up to West Point to talk to some American military historians there, which was fascinating. They were interesting, cultured, highly articulate people, very well-informed and a couple of them came to London to see *Taking Sides* but they didn't come to see me afterwards! Very significant! What they gave me was not necessarily what they thought they'd given me because I remember at one point we were looking out over the very beautiful Hudson River on which West Point sits and some extraordinary birds were flying across the river. I pointed at one of these and asked, 'Is that an eagle or a hawk?' My companion replied, 'Sir, I'm not an ornithologist, I'm a military historian.' That told me almost as much as I needed to know! There was an absolute speciality, a narrow focus about his interests. In some ways it was appropriate but I was as struck with that reply as I was with Arnold's utter indifference to music or, should I say, apparent indifference to music. I remember Harold Pinter, who directed the 1995 production, being pressed by a member of the audience who was insisting that Arnold is a complete philistine who understands nothing of music or culture. Harold Pinter said, 'Well, perhaps he does, it's just that he doesn't tell us he does.' His whole performance for the purpose of the interrogations is that of a philistine but he might go home and listen to Brahms. That's the mystery of dramatic character.

So did the fact that you'd played Arnold give you insights into playing Furtwängler?

It wasn't as significant as you might think. I still feel the play is finely balanced. There's a strong argument on both sides, hence its title. The difficulty in the theatre, of course, is that the representation of a persecuted artist automatically settles where the sympathies are likely to lie, especially with a largely middle-class theatre audience. You have a hard job as Arnold whatever you do to make his very believable case persuasive in the theatre – that is, that Furtwängler ruthlessly exploited his position with the Nazis for purposes of self-promotion. Furtwängler maintained that art and politics had no relation to each other and from Hitler's assumption of power in 1933 said that he wanted to demonstrate that art meant more than politics, which is why he stayed in Nazi Germany: he believed, as he says in the play, that through music he could preserve 'liberty, humanity and justice'. He argues that a single performance of a masterpiece is more powerful than the horrors of Auschwitz – and such a view is always going to win a certain kind of vote.

That claim is horrifically arrogant.

It is extraordinarily arrogant. The thing about Furtwängler is that he's not a natural hero. On the face of it, he's not an attractive man.

He was a supreme conductor but had all of that Prussian arrogance and the self-confidence that went with an old-fashioned maestro and I suppose to some extent still does. It's not as if he was a natural martyr or sympathetic victim. You have to get past a certain amount of conceit and high-handedness in him just as you have to get past a certain amount of foul-mouthedness in Arnold. To me the beauty of the play is that it hands it right back to you and says: what would you have done? What do you think? It's not answered for you, unlike some modern plays which tell you exactly what to think.

How did you research Furtwängler? I was looking at footage online and he had an extraordinarily dramatic style of conducting.

Yes, he was extraordinary looking too – his domed head, and his long, long neck like some strange bird and his almost simian arms. I spoke to a violinist in her nineties who had played under Furtwängler and said that no one in the orchestra ever knew when to come in because he waved his arms so much, and yet somehow you came in at the right place. He rarely gave the beat where it was expected. He was extremely suggestive, unlike Toscanini who was much more metronomic. There was a funny mixture of autocracy on the podium and trust in the musicians. Sometimes he wouldn't conduct them at all, he just trusted them to play with feeling and in time and then would return to his autocratic method again. The mixture of trust and control is fascinating.

Did you spend time studying Furtwängler's physicality?

I assume that your job affects your body. This was a man who spent his life conducting, which is taxing for the neck, shoulders and upper back. Every profession takes its toll on the body in certain ways so I had to find a physical disposition for him which suggested his *métier*. You don't do anything grossly exaggerated but you have to let that physicality dictate the way you walk, look and speak. I play him with a certain hauteur of manner.

I read in one source that he was verbally rather recalcitrant but that his writing was wonderfully fluid.

There's hardly any record of his spoken voice. We found one tiny recording of him introducing something to an orchestra and his timbre sounded dignified and fluent. There was nothing to be gained from my point of view from snatches of vocal material.

Did you work on his accent?

We did experiment with accent. The play proceeds on a tricky convention one has to accept – that the interrogation is being conducted in English and that Germans are speaking English, so there are traces of accent, some broader than others. The thing is confounded by history before you start – Furtwängler spoke no English at all.

Do you think there is a difference of psychological approach for the actor between the playing of a fictional character and the playing of a real one?

The issue here is that there must come a point when you stop researching. Research is fascinating, many actors love it, but there comes a point when you can hang by your own shoelaces. You can become obsessed by historical reality and lose your connection with the fictional world of the drama. You have to be clear that you are serving a play and that the priority is to find out how the play works. All that research gives you support and one would hope authenticity, but a historical narrative is not the same as a dramatic one. Ronald Harwood uses certain elements of Strauss's character and not others. Strauss was said to be a rather forbidding person when you first met him, but the Strauss in Ronald's *Collaboration* is extremely forthcoming and open most of the time. On the other hand, in the play he's almost always dealing with his family and close associates so you might expect him to be open. You don't see him in many circumstances in which he would need to be forbidding. There's a fork in the road, in other words, when the research is one thing and the play is another and that's true of any real character you play.

The other main consideration is tactical: how hard do you go towards physically suggesting a character? This very much depends on your assessment of how familiar your character is to your audience and what the risk might be of alienating them. In the case of Furtwängler the risk is medium, in the case of Strauss – medium. In the case of Charles Dickens, whom I played a year ago in Simon Gray's *Little Nell* (2007), the risk is not so high because Dickens is nineteenth-century and a bit more remote: we're familiar with his picture but there are no recordings of his voice. In the case of the media tycoon Robert Maxwell, whom I played in Ian Curteis's *The Bargain* (National Tour, 2007), the risk of alienating an audience was very high because most members of the public know exactly what he looked like and remember the stories attached to him. I had to go a long way to present a figure that looked like the photographs known to the public. Strauss was a medium risk because there aren't many people who were familiar with his appearance.

These days the devices we use in acting to make ourselves resemble someone are sophisticated. You can get fat suits like the one I wore to play Maxwell. You get fitted up to look exactly the right shape; it's like going to a Savile Row tailor – the precision of it is phenomenal. The sophistication of make-up and effects is even greater when you work in film. In the case of Maxwell you add the horrible shade of blue for your suit, your red tie, and find a way of reproducing his bushy eyebrows and you've pretty much got him. When you think of Chekhov you think of the beard and the glasses and the brow – I went to a lot of detail to get that exactly right in the television drama *A Wife Like the Moon* (1982) and for the one-man show I tour called *Anton Chekhov* (1984) and realised that, actually, three or four details do it for you. In the case of Furtwängler it seemed to me extraordinarily difficult to recreate that head. He was a strange-looking man and there were additional problems in that I'm in repertoire with another play so I couldn't go to great lengths to make myself look like him. I decided to play the character in a different body, if you see what I mean. With Strauss I think my resemblance is fairly good.

It seems to me that audience expectation is a factor you have to weigh up more carefully when you're playing a real person. The more prolific the images of a person, the higher the audience expectation that you must resemble them. But do you think audiences in theatre suspend disbelief more readily than film spectators?

I haven't thought about this before but I think you're right. In a movie like *The Queen*, a small number of actors were charged with playing extremely familiar figures and the camera gets in very close to their faces and bodies. It's difficult to pull off. I suspect more people come out of a film prepared to be openly critical if someone doesn't look like the person he or she is playing. I think for theatre audiences there is a greater sense of playfulness and a tolerance of what you might be up to as an actor. Theatre audiences are quite quick to note the decisions you have made in respect of playing the role and they travel with you. However, you don't want to encourage an attitude in the audience where they think they have to play detective and try to catch you out in the less convincing moments – that isn't the point.

I also wonder whether there is a quantum difference between a spectator who stays at home assessing the verisimilitude of an actor on TV and the small ritual of going out to the movies or the theatre; and I wonder whether, because you are making the effort to go somewhere else, you are willing to participate in a more generous way. Perhaps at home you are more of a passive audience and more inclined to criticise. I don't know but it's a thought.

Stellan Skarsgård, the actor who played Furtwängler in István Szabó's direction of Harwood's screenplay of *Taking Sides* (2001), didn't look like Furtwängler so that was obviously a decision made by the director, producer and actor. I don't think it counted against him at all, in spite of what we've just been saying, so I think this might be a more complicated territory than we think. In every actor's mentality there is a desire to surprise, a desire to dress up; you disguise yourself for your parents when you're five years old. You dip into your costume box and you hope they won't recognise you! There is a childlike quality in actors. There's something very absorbing about trying to suggest that you are someone else. The overarching point here is that you have to play real people far more now than you used to. For some reason, I don't know why, there are now far more roles of real people and fewer fictional roles. In the last few years I've played more historical people than I have before in my career – Oscar Wilde in Moisés Kaufman's *Gross Indecency: The Three Trials of Oscar Wilde* (1999), the curator and friend of the literati Sydney Cockerell in *The Best of Friends* by Hugh Whitemore (2006), George III in Alan Bennett's *The Madness of George III* (2003), Charles Dickens in 2007, and now Furtwängler and Strauss. I wonder sometimes if we are becoming less willing to embrace the imaginative.

With Furtwängler and Strauss have you made private decisions about their behaviour or what they stood for?

No, I've taken the Harwood line – I'm open-minded about it. Strauss grew up in a more innocent time than Furtwängler. His crisis in terms of the play happens right at the beginning of the Third Reich, from

1932 to 1934 when Hitler first came to power and when it was much more credible for someone like Strauss to believe that Nazism would blow over. In retrospect one has to be generous to his situation.

I've been very struck by the fact that all the actors we've interviewed have embraced the ambiguity of their characters.

You can only play a character from his or her own point of view and you must use all your tools, Stanislavski among them, to do that. To apply an external judgment about whether they are a good person or a bad person is completely beside the point. It's not for the actor to do because the character performing the actions isn't judging themselves. I think this is something that actors learn with time. I've sometimes heard an inexperienced actor say, 'I'm playing a cynical, nasty man', then of course you get the worst kind of 'adjectival' acting, when the actor plays general nastiness. But a nasty person does not necessarily know that they are nasty. Furtwängler ends up doubting himself and something in him from early on in the interrogation knows that there is a case to answer. He knows that he conducted under those huge Nazi flags for the Berliner Philharmonic Orchestra. Ronald doesn't refer to it in the play but Furtwängler also played for a great jubilee anniversary of the annexation of Czechoslovakia. He knows there is a moral question to answer, and Arnold, for all his coarseness and brusqueness, digs it out of him. Arnold suggests to him that the Jews Furtwängler saved might simply be his moral insurance policy. It's an intelligent point and whether Furtwängler acknowledges it or not, he knows that it is a point of view. As Arnold says: 'You're setting culture and art and music against the millions put to death by your pals?' In the end, Furtwängler breaks down just after Arnold's harrowing description of the camps and says that it would have been better if he'd left Nazi Germany.

Do you think historians and commentators have been hard on those who did not go into exile?

Perhaps. In those circumstances you live from one day to the next. You don't know what's going to happen and it's very hard to make judgments. Furtwängler says he should have left in 1934, but he leaves the room and the interrogation and continues with his career. Maybe he never says it again. There's one moment just after the terrible soul-searching and collapse when the secretary comes back, having seen him out, and reveals that he gave her his visiting card and asked her to have dinner with him! So the old Furtwängler comes out immediately after his terrible collapse. It's a dazzling moment, I think, and such moments make Ronald a great playwright. That's a good character point: he bounces back as he did in real life. He never played in America – there was great opposition to him – and the Americans never forgave him for staying in Nazi Germany. But I think the whole thing would have left a bigger mark on Steve Arnold because he has all the problems of the veteran returning to the States. He's seen the camps, which he can never forget. There are so many things he can never talk about. I think his life would have been more hobbled than Furtwängler's.

Yes, he's been seriously damaged.

An interesting thing about *Taking Sides* is that everyone in it is in *real* trouble. Nobody knows how long they will survive or how.

How does this contrast with playing Richard Strauss in Collaboration?

There's more sunlight in Strauss. He was a big baby in a way. He was an innocent and he was caught in a dreadful bind because the Nazi powers made him conscious of the fact that he should be very careful because he had a Jewish daughter-in-law, half-Jewish grandchildren, and that he really shouldn't make any trouble if he wanted them to be safe. What could be better designed as a threat to keep a person co-operating? It's another question for the audience. What would I have done to protect my grandchildren? – I might well have played ball. So he accepted Goebbels's appointment of him as President of the Reichsmusikkammer (the State Music Bureau) in 1933, saying that he would be 'apolitical'. In 1935 Strauss was forced to resign as President when he refused to remove his Jewish friend Stefan Zweig's name from the playbill for *The Silent Woman*. His daughter-in-law was placed under house arrest in 1938 and Strauss used his connections to release her. There is tremendous controversy about Strauss's role after the Nazi Party came to power. He was in an impossible position – both collaborator and dissident. In 1942 he moved back to Vienna where his family could be protected by the Gauleiter of Vienna. His reputation was more damaged by his apparent collaboration than Furtwängler's. I think he's still quite an ambiguous figure and many people say if it wasn't for *Metamorphosen* – a work composed to mark the bombing of Strauss's favourite opera house, the Hoftheater in Munich, and a piece which mourns the loss of pre-war European culture – his reputation would be very low indeed, despite his obvious genius. When he was arrested by American soldiers in 1945, it was his musical reputation which secured his protection.

I didn't know anything about Strauss and have been fascinated to make his acquaintance. What seems to make the play work is the calm before the storm – in the second half you really sense the shadows gathering. The first part deals with the period just after the Weimar Republic when it's possible for a great Jewish writer like Zweig to collaborate with Strauss, a great gentile German composer. The process of seeing that collaboration destroyed and of seeing Zweig destroyed and Strauss left devastated is what gives the play its force. I took some time to get onto terms with his music but I do see now that it is extraordinarily beautiful.

Did listening to the music of both composers give you any insights as an actor?

Partly, yes. With Furtwängler I can see that he's quite a radical. His experiments with the tempi and inflections were, even for someone like me who is not particularly adept at music, very interesting indeed. In the case of Strauss it took me a long time to get the melody. I had reason to get to know only one piece well, *The Silent Woman*: I play a tiny section on the piano. Just listening to it all the time has got me close to it and I'm beginning to see this rapturous, lyrical urge inside it. I find his world and his music immensely attractive in a way that I didn't before. I find his peculiar naïvety and the very single-minded lust to compose, which was his downfall because it made him either oblivious or indifferent to anything political at all, curiously attractive. This is the junction for both plays, isn't it – at what point does the artist take an interest in public life?

It's interesting to hear you say this. Just as you are fascinated by Strauss's naivety, a lot of critics come to the play and say it's unbelievable that an artist could really think that art and politics can be separated.

What's interesting about *Taking Sides* is how it generates discussion. Family and close friends fall out in the bar! It's a wonderful thing to see – as long as they make up afterwards! It really does divide people because this is a real, unresolved question for all of us: were these musicians morally bankrupt and craven or were they right to remain and write and to try to resist through their music? There are haunting lines at the end of *Taking Sides* when the younger American officer called David states: 'Only tyrannies understand the power of art. I wonder how I would have behaved in his position? I'm not certain I'd have "acted courageously". And what about you, Major? I have a feeling we might just have followed orders.' The Reich understood very well that Furtwängler and Strauss were important. In the Soviet Union, too, resistance was so often powerfully expressed in theatre and art in a way that it rarely is now. There is a fascinating relationship between despotism and the arts which is endlessly unresolved and of interest to us all. As we know, much great art has come out of oppression.

You've played a monarch – George III in The Madness of George III. *How did you get at the historical figure?*

What Alan Bennett has managed to do is what Shakespeare did: he filters our idea of a historical character through his own play. One no longer imagines Richard III as anything other than Shakespeare's picture of Richard III. When one thinks of George III one tends to think of Alan Bennett's play! I did research him and was struck by the number of wonderful things that he did that were nothing to do with the play. What's great about Bennett's drama is that it's like *King Lear* with a happy ending – he does recover, although he continued to have bouts of porphyria for the rest of his life. The moment when he inexplicably recovers is one of the most extraordinary moments I've ever had in the theatre – you can feel the audience's profound emotional relief. Nobody really knows what he sounded like or how he moved. There are just distant reports so in a sense that relieves you of the worry about historical accuracy. I did a routine amount of research to reassure myself that I was authorised to play the part.

What do you mean by 'authorised'?

You want to be legitimate. You want to be able to defend what you have done should you need to, so you do your research. Charles Dickens had a more familiar face to contemporary audiences than

George III so I worked on my appearance but I also read what his public readings were like. He was an extraordinary performer. He had great vocal and emotional range in that particular hybrid form, which is neither quite performing in a play nor quite reading from a lectern. He read in these claustrophobic auditoria and you sense that there was a sort of delirium in the audiences, which was partly to do with being in his presence and partly to do with being in these congested, gas-lit spaces. You try and suggest all this. I was trying to get more at physical likeness with Dickens than say, George III. It's more a form of acting, or a way of behaving where people are prepared to say: yes, I believe he might have been something like this. You always worry with any great writer or musician or anyone great: how do you play a genius? Well, how do you recognise a genius across a coffee table? You don't. A genius probably doesn't behave any more erratically or peculiarly than anyone else at first glance. But that's the question you have to engage with. How do you subliminally suggest that you are the person that could have written *Der Rosenkavalier* or *Great Expectations*?

How do you suggest that?

I don't know. It's the defensive challenge you set yourself.

We're getting into an area of acting that is very personal and instinctive and difficult to articulate.

Yes, you could say it's something to do with concentration. The very fact of people being alert to what you are attempting to do is galvanising. They positively want to believe it and in some mysterious way that makes it possible for you to do it.

INTERVIEWED BY MARY LUCKHURST, CHICHESTER,
6 AUGUST 2008

Siân Phillips

Playing Marlene Dietrich, Clementine Churchill, Emmeline Pankhurst, Mrs Patrick Campbell and Wallace Simpson

Siân Phillips played Marlene Dietrich in *Marlene* by Pam Gems (1996) in the West End, followed by an international tour. She also played Virginia Woolf in *A Nightingale in Bloomsbury Square* (Hampstead Theatre Club, 1973). On television she has played Livia in *I, Claudius* (1976); Emmeline Pankhurst in *Shoulder to Shoulder* (BBC, 1974); Clementine Churchill in *Winston Churchill: The Wilderness Years* (1981); and Wallis Simpson in *The Two Mrs. Grenvilles* (1987). Phillips has also appeared as the actress, Mrs Patrick Campbell, on television and stage, in *Jennie: Lady Randolph Churchill* (1974) and *Dear Liar* (Mermaid Theatre, 1982).

You've played quite a number of real people in your career.

I have. There is a general thing about playing real people which is that when they are dead you are off the hook (to a certain extent). When you are playing people who have died recently, or who are still alive, it is a nightmare. It is a ghastly responsibility for a start, because of families and descendents. There obviously is a limit to how far you can go to transform yourself into another person, with the best will in the world. Then the other major problem is that you can really only play the character if the writer writes appropriate scenes and lines for you. I've come unstuck in the past where the writer simply hasn't dealt in any depth with the character, so all my preparation went for nothing, apart from the appearance. One is very much at the mercy of the writer.

Does that affect your research?

Yes, absolutely. Take Livia in *I, Claudius* – very little is known about Livia. I did no research. I let the costume department do their job – their own research, I let the make-up people do their research, the wig department did theirs, and I didn't do any at all. I was playing a character in a play by one person, Jack Pulman, freely adapted from a novel written by another, Robert Graves, freely adapted from history! So I figured that all I could do was play Jack Pulman's story, which is a bit of a Jewish comedy. Also, there was very little time for research. I think we recorded the first episode two weeks after we first met! But the costume department had been working on it for about a year. Everything had been researched endlessly and was ready to go. Apart from us!

By contrast, Mrs Pankhurst was perhaps the character I researched the most. I worked on that project for about seven months. It was a period of history that I didn't know that much about when I started. At the BBC they lay out trestle tables in the rehearsal room and they put the reference books on them. In this instance it may have been a mistake because all of us girls suddenly became experts on that particular period of history, to the understandable irritation of the writer, Ken Taylor. He was a very good writer – but we kept finding scenes that we felt illuminated our own characters, so we asked him to put them in, and sometimes he did and it did work, but a lot of the time poor Ken had to cope with all these useless requests! (He *had* done a lot of research.) The costume department at the BBC is very good, so you always know you are going to look right (down to the buttons it will be right, the jewellery will be right). That is a great help, it gives one a lot of confidence.

Is company research of that kind unusual for television?

No, the BBC always does that when they are producing anything historical. Sometimes actors don't want to. Other times, as with the suffragettes, we got fascinated by the politics of the period and I think on the whole it paid off. But you have to realise that the writer makes the choices. Because something is spread out over seven episodes, seven hours of film over seven months, there is time for one to learn a lot and interfere! (In the theatre when you are given a play there is only a limited amount you can do.) The opposite of *Shoulder to*

Shoulder was *Winston Churchill: The Wilderness Years*. I *did* read up a lot about Clementine because I knew a bit about her anyway and I found her fascinating. I found their marriage fascinating. But it was of no use whatsoever because Martin Gilbert, who wrote the scripts, was not writing about Clemmie Churchill or about their marriage, but rather about Winston Churchill's problems in 'the wilderness years'. I was on screen a lot of the time but I was often just reacting to Winston. I was very embarrassed because I thought I wasn't doing her justice. I met Mary Soames (Clementine and Winston Churchill's daughter) afterwards and I was dreading that. I thought I had really short-changed her mother, but she was charming. I think she understood my predicament. I felt I could have done better but the writer didn't give me the tools.

Wallis Simpson was another real person I have played, this time for American television. I listened to a tape of her, and of course I had the wig! Oh the wig! The hair has to be right as you can imagine. It was a very well written script by Dominic Dunn, and the costumier, Cosprop, made me look thinner and shorter.

Virginia Woolf was interesting and I prepared hugely to play her. *A Nightingale in Bloomsbury Square* (1973) was a play by Maureen Duffy, who knew all about Virginia and the Bloomsbury Circle. I went on holiday to the Lake District and I took all of Woolf's diaries with me. I read them all during this holiday and I read biographies and letters. I also got a lot of her broadcasts from the BBC archive, so I had her voice as well. That was fascinating because of her delivery. I learnt her delivery and I found that it was very useful in Maureen's play as she had managed to capture the speech rhythms of Virginia Woolf. The play was more or less a monologue that lasted about an hour, so was a huge job of learning. Although they were not her actual words, the play was written in that tumbling sort of English they spoke. Of course, I couldn't use the heightened accent – even in the 1970s, it would have sounded absurd. It would have alienated the audience so much, it sounded affected and stupid – no one would have listened to it properly. So I had to use a version of her voice, but the rhythms were very useful even if I couldn't use her vowel sounds. I also worked quite hard on the wig. I'm a firm believer in wigs. I have a marvellous wig-maker Paul, and he managed to get that strange loopy hair that she had. It was really hard to figure it out. I know that it looked remarkably like her. I had clothes made too. I went to my dressmaker in Covent Garden and we recreated her clothes and shoes and so that helped. The surface can be important.

Is there a difference between theatre and television and film regarding the need for resemblance?

I think you can accomplish more in the theatre because you are further away! When I played Mrs Patrick Campbell on stage I remember I had a wonderful wig, and the clothes were great. However, I realised if I imitated her I would get into difficulties. People who imitate her do so in the same way that they imitate Dame Edith Evans – they give her a booming voice. (All the stories that are told about Mrs Pat are done so in that deep actressy voice.) But she didn't talk at all like that. I heard an old tape of her and her voice was quite light and very quick. So again, I had to steer a middle course. Sometimes you can give people what they want, but sometimes you can't. When I played Mrs Pat on TV I looked less like her, but of course that was in close-up.

The person I lived with longest was Marlene, and that was also the most difficult because she was recently dead. People have seen her perform. Her children are alive, her daughter, her grandchildren. A lot is known about her. She is also one of the most glamorous women in the world, which presents another problem! As Pam Gems says in the play, she is a creature of superlatives. It was agony starting – I didn't want to start. My agent talked me into it. I had done a musical some years before that and because I hadn't sung before my voice was very, very low. Apparently it sounded exactly like Marlene's voice, and that is the reason people said I should play her. So I had the wig-maker who had made her wigs make my wig, including a special bit on the front that was knotted differently so that when she bowed, it dropped down. (Things like that were fascinating to learn.) The person who made my dress copied the original design. All the beading was correct, down to the number of glass pendants. The material around the chest and the arms was meant to look like skin, but it wasn't; it was a material you can only get in Paris. The lighting man got his lighting plot from her tour, so the help I had was gigantic. The famous coat, of course, is made from feathers, not fur. I also met lots of people who knew her, and a lot of people gave us actual dialogue to put in the play. But finally my way into it was through the music. It was her singing voice. The musical director and I spent months alone together listening to her singing until we could reproduce her phrasing, her breathing. The assistant director, Thierry Harcourt, knew a lot about her and got me all the footage of her press conferences, her arrival in airports, all those things. We sat for weeks looking at this material until we got the walk right. We sat and did all that surface stuff, and in the end it became an intrinsic part of the character. It is a way into character, from the surface. We copied every finger movement, every gesture on every note she sang. My director would sit opposite me. (He knew it backwards.) But goodness it was so laborious, I can't tell you. In a way, though, that's how I got myself into the part. I never saw myself in the dress or the wig. It was a quick change in the wings. I just had to trust the dressers to get me into it and throw me on to the stage. I know that people used to get a bit of a turn when the curtain rose.

It was very touching because a lot of people who used to work with her came to see the show. Her sound man came, he was such a quiet man, and was in tears when he came round to see me after. He said he was so pleased because he had never seen her show from the front before. You see everything is now done from the back of the auditorium, but back then the lighting and sound would be operated from the wings. I knew the concert was accurate. That was very satisfying. I had to forget I was pretending to be someone so famous. I had to stop being so intimidated and just get on with it.

I was once directed by Samuel Beckett in *Eh Joe*. That was a challenge because he taps his finger like a metronome and you have to count the full stops, commas, semi-colons, they all counted. So preparing a text with him is a purely mechanical and tortured affair. You have no contribution of your own at all. You are a machine trying to do it. Lots of actors won't do it, but I got it into my head that I would stick it out and see where it went. In the end, I realised it was the only way to do the play. It became second nature – I couldn't imagine doing it any other way. The mechanical work suddenly became real, became personal, it was very strange. But the point is that the same happened with Marlene, the external, the minute details one worked on didn't feel at all useful and then suddenly it all came together and one feels like someone else.

Did playing Marlene start with Pam Gems's completed script?

No, not at all. I was working with Pam Gems on Ibsen's *Ghosts* and my agent suggested that she would be the perfect person to write Marlene, and that I should mention it to her. So I asked her if she'd be interested and within a few months this script came through. It didn't have the final shape, but the National Theatre gave us the money to workshop it for three weeks, and we did it as a promenade production, so the audience walked with me through this big studio theatre, and we visited different scenes in her life. It was like a 'happening' (it was to be a strange kind of 'event'). So then I started working on the music with Kevin Amos who was the musical director, and it became more formal and we realised that the concert at the end was a good thing to aim for. So it became a backstage dressing-room story which then transformed into a cabaret performance. Obviously, Marlene's dialogue is Pam's invention, but we both talked to a lot of people, and much of what they told us went in. There is a scene in the play in which she instructs the ushers exactly how and when to give her flowers at the end of the play. That was all given to me by Keith Baxter, who saw her rehearsing at Golders Green with Binkie Beaumont when she was teching the show in. I told Pam and she put it straight in. There were many things like that. Lighting – she always used to light herself. She knew if there was one lamp that was not quite right. (She could also tell if one instrument was slightly off, as she was a very good musician, she trained as a violinist.) The last line before I go on stage was given to us by a great friend of hers that travelled with her (she got her friends to do jobs for her on tour rather than pay people), she told us that Marlene was ready to go on stage and she turned and said to her, 'let's see if we can fool them one more time'. I asked her if I could use it. It was the same with her make-up, I got sent make-up she hadn't used, her assistants sent me some lashes, they were folded round a pencil so they could be re-used (she was very economical!). I had so many things of hers, and so many letters of hers that she would write to directors. All these things helped me.

There is a section in the play in which she talks about Germany and becoming an American citizen.

Pam made that up. We were told by her daughter that we couldn't use one word of her book or we'd be sued. But the play is a work of the imagination. It never happened that she sat in the dressing room and said these things. Pam must be a terrific 'guesser' as people would come round and tell me that they couldn't understand how she knew certain things, and of course she didn't, she made them up. Pam has the great writer's skill of being able to get inside someone else's mind.

Were there any particular images of her you wanted to capture?

Oh the walk, the look, the whole thing. Not so much in the first half of the play. (Even with the wig on I couldn't really look like her.) But with the dress, the wig and the voice in the cabaret I could look enough like her. The most I could do was to ensure the last half-hour was accurate. But you see, I didn't have to worry about the first half as much because nobody would know whether it was accurate or not. They only knew what she was like publicly.

How do you go about capturing the charisma or star quality of Marlene?

There has to be something. But it is too hard to pin it down. You can't be that other person, it is impossible. You have to do all your research until you know the person very, very well, and then you just have to jump off the cliff and hope for the best. Worrying about it is about the worst thing you can do.

Did you continue to talk to Pam throughout the process?

Yes, all the time. It got re-written endlessly, and continued to be re-drafted on the tour. It was an endless process! Pam really is an amazing writer. I couldn't have given that performance without the script. Without the material you can't convey any of the things you need and want to convey.

Did your view of her change from playing her?

Yes, it did. I saw her perform at Wimbledon in the 1970s, it was one of her last ever stage performances. I have to admit I had not been terribly interested in her as an actress. (I was more interested in those days in the Swedish stars like Ingrid Thulin.) I don't think many of the film scripts were good either. But I saw the cabaret and I was very interested then! It was incredible. She's one of the few people whose career in my opinion got better as she got older. She was an average actress but she was a magnificent cabaret performer. So my opinion changed, because I knew she was self-obsessed (tediously self-obsessed) I thought that she wasn't a person that I would particularly like, but my respect for her grew hugely. I was amazed that she managed to go out there and do her show for so long, with her bad legs and the pain.

Of course we haven't talked about the fact that you are a performer playing a performer. Did you therefore have a greater understanding of her?

Yes, I think so. As I say, I came to admire her hugely and it is to her performance I owe my cabaret career. I've been doing cabaret for ten years, all over the world. That is because people came to see that play and thought I was a cabaret performer.

Is your cabaret similar to Marlene's?

Well not really because I talk to the audience and she never talked. The whole thing was extremely controlled, always the same. There was nothing spontaneous.

You said in an interview that you wouldn't describe what you were doing as impersonation.

Well, I suppose it was. The play wasn't but the concert was – it had to be. I never felt that was demeaning in any way. I really tried to copy her as accurately as I could. That was hard enough!

More generally, when playing a real person do you think there is a difference in your approach? Something different psychologically?

Yes, but it is very difficult to describe. Trying to analyse the process, one starts making no sense whatsoever. When you play a real person you can't let too much of yourself seep through, and that requires a lot of concentration. You can bend a fictional character to resemble yourself. You can't do that with real people.

INTERVIEWED BY TOM CANTRELL, MANCHESTER,
19 MARCH 2009

Elena Roger

Playing Eva Peron and Edith Piaf

Elena Roger played Eva Peron in *Evita* by Andrew Lloyd Webber and Tim Rice (Adelphi Theatre, London, 2006) and Edith Piaf in Pam Gems's *Piaf* (Donmar Warehouse and West End, 2008), for which she won an Olivier Award.

How did your involvement in Evita *start?*

I am the first Argentinean actress to play Eva Peron in London. It is naturally quite easy for me to play an Argentinean – I know how it works! In England when you have a dinner party you talk about the weather, whereas in Argentina you talk about politics. I remember all the lunches and dinners with my family when we would discuss politics for hours. My father would debate and argue with my mother, or sometimes they would just scream at each other, arguing the same thing, but still screaming passionately. They talked about Peron and the military period.

Eva was an iconic political figure. I suppose she was an unusual First Lady. She came from a very humble background, but had dreams of being a film actress; she had found some success on the radio when she met Peron in 1944. At this stage he was a Colonel in the army. He was much older than Eva (she was born in 1919; he in 1895). There was big political change in Argentina in the 1940s. Peron rose through the ranks of the army and became President in 1946. Eva was very important to his success both as Peron's First Lady, but also in her own right. She was very popular with the working classes and ran the Ministries of Labour and Health. In 1947, she created the Eva Peron Foundation, which provided many social services including education programmes and women's suffrage (which was granted in 1947). They were incredibly popular with the Argentinean people.

Eva's health began to fail as her husband was re-elected for his second term in 1951. She died of cancer in 1952, aged 33. Peron did not complete his second term – he lost power following a military coup in 1955. He returned to power in 1973, but died a year later. He left his third wife, Isabel Martinez, as President, which was quite a disaster for my country. Maybe it was because she wasn't like Evita, but for whatever reason, it was a big problem. Isabel was deposed in a military coup in 1974, leaving my country facing de-industrialisation, recession and endemic corruption. Evita is therefore still an iconic figure in Argentina.

Although there was some teaching about these periods in school, most of what I learnt about the Perons was from home, from my mother and father who knew about them from their own experience of living in the country at the time. I have since read some textbooks that were used in schools when the Perons were in power. They taught phrases to young children, there would be sentences like, 'I love my mother and my father, Evita loves me, Peron loves me.' I thought, oh my God!

So when I was cast in *Evita*, I started researching them and learning more about the history of my country. I read the books, I watched the documentaries. My dance training focused on corporeal expressiveness. The physical side of performance comes naturally to me.

Where did you train?

When I was a child in Buenos Aires we didn't have musical theatre schools. So I started dancing at a local club, but it shut down. When I was about eight, after a year of not being able to have lessons, I begged my mother to find me a dance teacher. I was lucky, my mother found an amazing teacher. I had lessons twice a week, one day an hour of Spanish dance, classical dance and an hour of jazz. Then on the other day instead of Spanish we had tap. I did that for ten years, adding courses on salsa, contemporary dance and tango. I spent more and more time in that club dancing. When I was in high school I didn't enjoy my academic studies as much as dance – that was all I wanted to do. It was then I started singing, only for an hour a week though. When I finished high school I went to the

National Conservatory of Music in Buenos Aires, and I studied singing and piano. Before I finished the course I started working professionally in the theatre. I started working in 1995, and in 2000 I started going to acting classes in between jobs. All those classes I took were eye-opening, as I realised I had a lot of study to do, lots of books to read about acting. I needed to watch more films, more theatre – it is hard to believe it now, but I didn't go to the theatre. I started reading history and learning more languages. It is all useful, it all builds.

So how much about the details of Evita's life did you know before you started working on the play? Was it new research?

It wasn't new, no. I knew a lot about her, but I realise that we will never know the truth about anything. Particularly political figures. The more I read on Evita, the more I became aware of the agendas, some for Peron and Eva's leadership, others against. Every biographer has a point of view. They all have their own political agenda, their own take on Evita's career. I found just one of the books quite balanced – where she is presented as both good and bad. I read all the truths and lies about Evita, and of course the play is another lie.

Did you know the play before you became involved?

Only the song 'Don't Cry for me Argentina'.

What was your initial response to the play?

Well, it was clear that some scenes were completely imagined events, that they were pure fiction. So I just followed my feelings about the character through the play. It was very important to my approach to playing her that she believed in what she was both doing and saying. I wanted to play Evita as a real person. I wanted her to believe what she was saying. I know that some of the lines in the play are written as if she was not telling the truth, so I had to use some irony, and it is also possible that she was manipulated by Peron, but I think she had belief in her words. That integrity was very important to me.

Did you meet and talk to Andrew Lloyd-Webber about the production?

Yes I did. He used to come to the rehearsal room to correct some of the musical details, and he made some cuts just before the opening night.

I also met Tim Rice. I have a good relationship with him. He went to Buenos Aires just after Peron died, in 1974, to research the play when he was writing the lyrics, which impressed me. When he started writing this play (which premiered in London in 1978), there were very few documentaries, and everything was very hidden because, as I said, it was in the middle of a very bad period in the country. I think he did it very well, as he couldn't do a lot of research from England, he actually visited. Tim told me that when he was a child he used to collect stamps, and the most beautiful ones had Evita Peron's face on them. He thought that she was so beautiful, and so she stuck in his mind.

So did you do your research before rehearsals, or was this during them?

No, I started before, because I knew my rehearsal period was going to be very busy. I wanted to know everything before. But I didn't have that much time – I knew I was going to be Evita at the end of January 2007 and we started rehearsing at the beginning of April, so I didn't have long to read a lot!

I watched many documentaries. When I watched them, one of the things I noticed was the passion of the crowd, and the body language of the people listening to Eva speak. One of the most incredible and beautiful things that happened to me when I was playing Evita was that I started to see this body language in the actors during her public speeches. We have the phrase '*pueblo*', the crowd. I think that is something quite specific to her era – the way the crowds reacted.

Before the rehearsals began I also watched the film version with Madonna, mainly to see how it was structured as a musical, to see how it all fits together.

So when you looked at the archive film footage of Eva were there certain things you were looking for?

It was the speeches. I believe that both the thoughts and the movements of the actor must work together. You have to believe in your thoughts to establish the right movement. This is why I wanted her to believe in what she said. I am a dancer so it is quite easy for me to identify and copy body details. I think of all movement as choreography. I have a visual memory. I am also quite a clown, so I have a good physical awareness and freedom. When I saw her giving speeches, there were a few things I noticed: firstly her hands, she did something strange with her hands, she held her fingers at a certain angle, there was tension in them. Musical theatre isn't film, I didn't want to just copy. I wanted to understand the particular strength and energy which would make someone hold their fingers like that. What mattered was to understand her physicality, copying her was not the point.

Did you also research the era in the rehearsal periods as a company?

A lot of research was done during rehearsals as a company. Michael Grandage [Director], Jamie Lloyd [Associate Director], Catherine Totti [Resident Director] researched a lot and Ana Moll [assistant to Patrick Murphy, Head of Production] provided a lot of books and documentaries about Argentina. We watched some videos during rehearsals, and we looked at photographs too.

I remember one exercise which was very helpful. Michael Grandage asked everybody in the company to choose a name. Individual actors often played more than one character, some were military, some were workers, so they had to choose one of them and give them an Argentinean name. Everyone then had to make up a story about that person, and give their viewpoint of the period. That was great, because it meant that the whole cast had to understand the history and start to imagine what it was like for different people doing different jobs.

We also researched the *pueblo*. I suppose that every *pueblo*, every crowd in each country will have some similarities, but we wanted to make it specific. For example, in England you have had a lot of wars. We haven't had as many, but we have had different things, we had a period when the country was run by the military, in South America we have had recent revolutions, and we are part of a third-world continent. Life in a third-world country is very different from life in a first-world country. We talked about how this might affect the people, the *pueblo*. Michael Grandage gave a lot of attention to detail.

You also played the legendary singer Edith Piaf in Pam Gems's play Piaf *in the West End. What was your initial feeling about being cast in the production?*

I was very scared, because of everything I had to learn, particularly the French, but also I had to act, speaking without the help of music.

It is easier with music, I think. It helps the audience relax; it sets the mood. The focus on the text is a striking feature of British theatre. British actors are trained to perform text to high standards, so with my dance background it was very intimidating. I felt everyone had 'technique'. So coming here to act was very nerve wracking!

What did you know about Edith Piaf before you took the project on?

Not that much. My mother liked her music, so I knew some of her songs, but I didn't know much at all about her as a person. I had to study. I took a train to Paris a couple of times. Before I went, I read a biography and wrote down all the important addresses in her life – these were the places I needed to visit. I went to her house where she was born, I went to the cemetery she is buried in, I went to the Olympia Theatre where she used to perform, I went to the Champs Elysees where she had a house, and to the Gerny's Club where she performed for the first time. I didn't speak to anyone who used to know her, because I can't speak much French. I took some photographic material with me and I walked around Paris. I went to the Edith Piaf Museum in Paris, which has all her things. The curator showed me some of her films, I didn't know that she was an actress too: she was in four or five films. She worked with Jean Cocteau on *The Human Voice* (1930). It is an amazing monologue. I felt that going to Paris alone, and walking down the streets she walked down, was very helpful. I started to imagine her in her own environment, I felt I started to understand her. I drank in the atmosphere. It also reminded me how poor people in those areas must have lived; how they cleaned their bodies, how they cooked, how they begged. We are used to having basic things, food, a bed, a house, particularly in the UK, which is a rich country. It was very different for Piaf. In all my acting work I have continued to observe, to read, to travel – the more you can understand people and the way they live, the better your work on stage.

Did you ever find that when you had done your research, and went back to the play, there were any decisions that the writer had made that you disagreed with?

Yes, sometimes, and the director changed some things. A good director will listen to your questions. With Jamie Lloyd [the director of *Piaf*], we discussed moments, and if we only needed to change a word here or there, we did it, but if there were more major changes, he talked to Pam Gems. Prior to rehearsal a lot was cut by Pam Gems for the production.

Was recreating Piaf's distinctive voice a technical challenge?

No, when I sing in her range, my voice is quite similar. I didn't try to copy it sound for sound. I have tried to copy her 'r', which is quite guttural. The fact that I am singing in French and with Piaf's accent, deceives you into believing that you are hearing Piaf. It helps that there is no interval. Audiences are captive in their seats, and are drawn in to the play from the beginning. They are never released from their engagement with the play. If it goes well, they share the same space, the same journey and they start dreaming. They believe that I am Piaf.

Even though she had such a distinctive voice, I don't think of my portrayal as an imitation. We have videos and CD recordings for that. I do something different. It might start with an imitation, but it has to be real, it has to be alive. If I don't believe what I am doing, live on stage, it is only an imitation of her words. And that is not interesting. I am doing more than that. The thing is to make the audience believe you are living in the moment.

Do you find it physically demanding, performing such a harrowing role for eight performances a week?

It is very demanding. You find out very quickly how to take care of your body. I rest a lot during the day. I don't speak too much by phone, I don't shout or scream. I have a good diet, and drink a lot of water. You are constantly focused on how to keep going.

Was Piaf's physicality a way in to playing her, or did you start with the voice?

With Piaf it was both together. However, it was very important to establish the different physicalities for the periods of her life. In the play she has a car crash, has three ribs removed, and develops a morphine addiction, so it was important to make decisions about how weak my body had to be in each scene and why. It could be that she has a car crash, but she still has her strength, later she might be in a wheelchair, but has enough energy to talk. I had to decide when her hands started to be disfigured from the arthritis. When she is sad, she assumes one posture, when she is happy, another.

Was this progression something which you discussed with the director?

No, I experimented with different physicalities and asked the director for feedback.

Has your view of both characters changed through playing them?

Yes, it has changed a bit. When you are playing them you have a bond with them, you think about them, and live with them every night for weeks!

Did it make a difference that these two women were real people?

Well, I was quite lucky that when I played Fontine in *Les Miserables*, although [she] was not a real person, Victor Hugo's description in the book is so specific, that you can imagine everything about her life. Evita and Edith were real, but you still have to imagine a lot of things. As I said, both scripts are different from her actual life – the writer has to invent a lot of things so you had to imagine how the real person would act in these fictional scenes. But I could watch their energies in the video material. The real job of the actor is about observation: to observe all the time, everything and everybody. Then you have more things to play with. Because I was a dancer, and then started singing, I didn't really study acting, so I had to have a lot of acting classes later. I also learnt a lot from appearing on stage. I didn't have a strict actor training. I just do what feels right. You have to believe in your actions, if you do, you can rely on your instincts. For me it is all about instinct and observation.

Interviewed by Tom Cantrell, London,
4 November 2008

Timothy West

*Playing Winston Churchill, Joseph Stalin, Mikhail
Gorbachev, Sir Thomas Beecham and John Bodkin Adams*

Timothy West played Winston Churchill in *Churchill and the Generals* (BBC, 1981), *The Last Bastion* (1984) and *Hiroshima* (1995); Joseph Stalin in David Pownall's *Masterclass* (Old Vic, 1983); Mikhail Gorbachev in *Breakthrough at Reykjavik* (Granada TV, 1987); Sir Thomas Beecham in *Beecham* (YTV, 1990); and serial killer John Bodkin Adams in *The Good Doctor Bodkin Adams* (BBC, 1986).

You once said you'd become known as the actor who plays real people.

Yes, I'm not sure what started that. I've played many actual people from Edward VII to Churchill, Gorbachev, the dictator Joseph Stalin, the conductor and impresario Sir Thomas Beecham, the suspected serial killer John Bodkin Adams, the artist William Morris, and I'm just about to fly to South Africa to play the politician P. W. Botha for a television drama.

Did you feel that it was a problem that you were known for playing real people?

I'm not keen on any designation. It's constricting and it doesn't make sense. There isn't a type of real person. All real people are as different as unreal people.

Where do you start with playing someone like Churchill?

Ian Curteis's screenplay, *Churchill and the Generals*, was the first time I played Churchill and I've played him three times since. When it's a historical person you start by seeing what you can lay your hands on. When it's a celebrated person you often have the great advantage of being able to find out a lot about them: you can look at pictures or paintings, more recently photographs, film footage, and you might listen to voice tapes. There are also people's personal recollections but those are a bit dangerous because they are so subjective. You always have to remember that you are not playing the person as he was historically, any more than you are in Shakespeare where you are playing Henry V, but as the playwright wants you to think of him. You're tied quite properly to the text and the author's view. Anything which is true, unless it is destructively contrary to the text, is very good background material. If you're playing a fictitious person you can be more inventive in terms of their offstage life.

The general public tends to have formed iconic constructions of celebrated, historical figures. There must be all sorts of decisions to be made about how you play that figure in the private realm.

You have to invent it. Churchill is a good example: what we associate with him publicly is his mastery of rhetoric, his creation and delivery of the great speeches. But that is not the mode he would have used to ask his wife, Clemmie, for a cup of tea. You have to find a distillation of that public figure, to reduce and naturalise it. You have to convince the audience that you've done your homework, visually and vocally. You have to be consistent, of course, and you have to strike memorable chords in the audiences' minds.

What were the memorable chords you chose for Churchill?

Vocally, Churchill used particular kinds of cadences which I think were probably not natural but which he found useful. It's not a bad idea to suggest that they became part of a persona he wanted to project and he used them in everyday speech as well. He found it more effective to deploy a falling cadence at the end of a line rather than a rising one – it makes the sound less, shall we say, effortful; it reduces artifice. It was very effective, I think. He understood how to attract the public's trust through particular techniques of oral delivery.

The whole thing of having to look like a person can be carried too far. When I first got the part the American co-producer was worried that I didn't look anything like Churchill, and it's true, I don't. So we went through an enormously elaborate make-up process. I had my hair bleached white, and a hair-piece made. I had a false nose. I had false ears, something I'd never dreamed of! I spent hours in the make-up chair every morning. The thing that really bugged me were the blue contact lenses. If you have brown irises, the blue lenses have to be of a greater expanse than your irises otherwise you see a brown rim. You feel as if you are looking down a tunnel and it's very disorientating and unnerving. The optician told me: 'Avoid bright lights and cigarette smoke.' 'I'm on a film set for ten hours a day and continuously smoking a cigar', I told him. 'Well, good luck!', he said. But as if that's not bad enough, in close-up I thought the effect made me look as though I was wearing a mask. I thought it was a great mistake. When I next played the role in Australia for a film called *The Last Bastion* (1984) the make-up artist was not inclined to repeat those excesses and he was quite right. The point I'm making is that the audience trust you if you make a few key gestures towards the visual image. The cigar is important as is the blue-spotted bow-tie, various hats were significant, but apart from that, if people think you've taken the trouble they will accept your version. The impressionist Rory Bremner achieves remarkable make-up and voice transformations for a quick snapshot of people. For a two-hour play, though, this would be inappropriate and actually destructive.

What was your vignette of Churchill?

I think it's psychological. The interesting thing about Ian Curteis's script, in my view, was that it explored the idea that Churchill was always the victim of his own instincts. He often preferred his own instincts to any advice that was being fed to him by his expert generals and politicians during the Second World War. This sometimes led him to make disastrous mistakes, like the Dardanelles campaign, and sometimes it helped to win the war. Once you decide that this is the thing motoring him, you have to try and explain it to the audience. His capacity to go against the counsel of highly qualified advisors frightened him. A small part of his mind knew that it was a perilous thing but he couldn't stop himself. You act with that thought in your mind.

Can you allow public assumptions, say, of Stalin or Gorbachev, to play any part in your construction of a role?

No. You're playing what the playwright wants you to play. Both these figures were, of course, outside my nation and culture but you still do your research. I played Gorbachev for a television play, *Breakthrough at Reykjavik*, about the Reykjavik arms talks: the drama explored how Ronald Reagan, the President of America, and Gorbachev, the last Head of State of the USSR, came at the talks from different angles. Gorbachev's policies of *perestroika* and *glasnost* contributed to the end of the Cold War, and he later won the Nobel Peace Prize. His international standing was immense, but his domestic image sustained irreparable damage. I examined news footage and analysed what they said, trying to work out whether they were saying what they meant, or whether they were using political ploys, or perhaps a combination of both.

Did you speak to historians?

Yes, but that can, of course, be confusing because you hear contrary views. You pick up different information from different people – without knowing it someone might give you a detail which provides you with a real key to how you might play it.

I think Gorbachev was a very genuine man. I think he had a wonderful gift for trying to smooth over various international difficulties. He was extraordinary at analysing his adversaries, as was Reagan. That's what was so fascinating about the whole confrontation. Reagan had developed a rather stuttering, bumbling persona which he used to disguise the fact that he was as sharp as a pin. They were both very astute politicians. It would have been very difficult to find out about Gorbachev as a private man but I didn't really need to know that, it wasn't appropriate. You have to guess. For the voice, I listened to him very carefully.

What about Stalin?

I played Stalin in David Pownall's black comedy *Masterclass* in 1983. It's based on a meeting, which may or may not have happened, in the Kremlin in 1947, between Stalin, Zhdanov – the cultural minister – and the composers Shostakovich and Prokofiev. Stalin was responsible for the death of millions in the USSR in the mid-twentieth century through economic hardship, famine and political purges. In the play Stalin is trying to get the composers to write the kind of music that will encourage people to work harder, make them love the Communist Party more, and make them politically happy. The play asks whether a restrictive government that cares about art is necessarily any worse than a liberal government that doesn't begin to care about art. Stalin was represented as a wonderful politician, a manipulator of people but possessed of a terrible sentimentality. He was extraordinarily devious. I talked to a diplomat who had attended an all-night gathering with Stalin. Everyone was drinking an alarming amount and becoming increasingly drunk. Stalin was drinking from his own special bottle and when he temporarily left the room a group decided to give it a try, assuming that it was very expensive vodka that he didn't want to share. In fact, it was water. He was simply acting drunk but doing it entirely convincingly and for political advantage.

Stalin's voice was more complicated to find than Gorbachev's. The four people onstage in *Masterclass* were all Russian, but we didn't want to do the whole play in Russian accents. The other three figures were from Moscow. Stalin was from Georgia and proud of it, he often played on it, in fact. I listened to a Georgian accent and compared it to a Muscovite accent. I found the differences in pronunciation and then applied them to English so I gave him a sort of Russian accent but using particular Georgian inflections. It wouldn't have worked in a straight English accent. It may have sounded like a 'stage' Russian accent but it worked for me.

Were there any objections to you playing a dictator as notorious as Stalin?

I got some letters, yes. I hope it didn't emerge as a sympathetic portrait. I didn't feel it was. You laugh at him. One of the funniest scenes I've ever played in my life was the attempt to write a song cycle by committee, but at the same time Stalin was a man who could make your blood run cold. I hope that audience members were wondering, as they watched the play, whether those two composers were going to be granted permission to continue to write music or whether they were going to be taken away and shot.

How do you try to convey that sense of power?

You have to believe that you have power over life and death, that you can command instant execution – of anybody.

Have you ever disagreed with an author over a line or a role?

David Pownall was very easy to engage in discussion. You could ask him for help, consult him about whether you had it right or not, ask him to convince you on a point. In film you don't have time for those discussions! You have to make it work. It's no good playing something that you don't believe in. You have to convince yourself that you have thought certain thoughts and the audience have to believe that too – it's the essence of acting really. You draw your thought-line, which may include deviations that aren't apparent to the audience at all, but as long as the audience believe in your psychological portrait, you're fine.

You've just used an interesting image. Do you write out your thought-line?

About half way through rehearsal I go through the part, reading it to myself, and study it not just from line to line, but from moment to moment. I examine all my thoughts. I consider what has happened in a particular moment to make me think differently. Then at the end of the play, when I've got the whole thought-line, I ask myself: is it true? Have I really thought all these thoughts or am I evading something? If I've convinced myself that it's all 'true' – a word I use a lot – I read it again, asking myself if it is clear. Will the audience be muddled? If I'm convinced on a second reading that it is both true and clear, I read the script again and ask myself whether it is interesting. It's no use going for truth and clarity if it isn't also going to be worth watching or listening to. Is it true? Is it clear? Is it interesting? In that order. When I've satisfied myself on all these counts, I go on.

That's a very compact description of your process.

I think I'd been doing this unconsciously for years, then I articulated it to someone once and realised that I had more of a systematic analytical process than I'd thought. Actors don't talk to each other very much about their own ways of working. I think many are quite private about it. If something has cropped up in a play which everybody finds is affecting the scene, we might go to the pub and hack it about, but otherwise how you work on your own is your own business.

You made an interesting point earlier on about the consciousness with which celebrated figures play roles and are themselves actors, of a kind.

Indeed. Most people with highly public roles have a dimension as a performer. Politicians, of course, aspire to performance, especially close to elections.

We remember the conductor and wit, Sir Thomas Beecham, as a flamboyant performer, but underneath it he was a man of private passions, especially when it came to women. He liked to project an image which he knew would help to popularise classical music. He was the first British conductor to have a sustained international career and he founded both the London Philharmonic and Royal Philharmonic Orchestras.

How do you find the physicality of a role?

I pick on particular traits and images of a person and try to find a way of playing them, particularly early on in the play. Sometimes it's more important than others. For Beecham I was mostly sitting on the conductor's podium, talking to the orchestra. It was a theatrical two-hander performed as a tribute to him. I had a very clear image of how he used to sit, based on an instinct. I think I must have got somewhat obsessive about it but I got the carpenter to lower the stool by three inches and then I realised the rail I was leaning on was the wrong height too. Finally I got it right and two musicians who had been conducted by Beecham wrote to me and told me that I had got the physical image exactly right.

You must have had an astonishingly accurate memory.

I'd hardly ever seen him perform. I don't know what it was. I'd retained something – Beecham's ghost perhaps, or divine intervention! I can't rationalise it.

Another example would be playing Stalin, who'd had polio as a child and didn't have the use of his left hand. He had to do everything with his right hand. People ask, 'do you take your performance home with you at night?' Of course I don't, but a specific physical trait like that needs practice so it's good to get used to doing things with one hand. If you make a striking image in the play early on which the audience associate with the collective memory of that person, then they will place their trust in you.

Presumably physical restrictions like that affect the psychology of the character you develop too?

Yes, definitely. Stalin was very quick to take offence. If anyone accidentally offered him a glass on his left-hand side that person could be marked for life, or perhaps death. It can work the other way round. I've been reading up on P. W. Botha: his obsession with Nelson Mandela overturned his rational approach to politics and eventually brought on a stroke from which he never recovered.

What about the psychology of a serial killer?

I played the suspected serial killer John Bodkin Adams in a television drama and found it absolutely fascinating. He was a general practitioner in Eastbourne and in 1957 he was tried for the murder of one of his patients. More than 160 of his patients died in suspicious circumstances, but police couldn't produce any hard evidence of what they suspected was enforced euthanasia and he got off. It was a sensational court case and became known as one of the greatest murder trials of all time. As it happens my father had been treated by him for sunstroke and recollected that he was a charming man, extremely helpful and devoted to his patients. There were scores of similar testimonies and he was renowned in the town for his care of the elderly. But there was also testimony that he'd arrived at the house of a female patient the day after her death and asked her relatives whether she'd left him the car or the silver. When they responded that they didn't know, he said he'd take the typewriter. It was an intriguing challenge to play a man who was remembered in such extremely diverse ways: unspeakably ruthless to some and terribly nice to the majority. They say that truth is stranger than fiction but this is the sort of profound paradox that playing a real person can offer up and it's an extraordinary and highly stimulating test of your ability.

INTERVIEWED BY MARY LUCKHURST, LONDON,
21 MAY 2008

Selected Further Reading

Atkinson, Tiffany. *The Body* (Basingstoke: Palgrave Macmillan, 2005).

Auslander, Philip. *Presence and Resistance: Postmodernism and Cultural Politics in Contemporary American Performance* (Ann Arbor: University of Michigan Press, 1994).

Auslander, Philip. *Liveness: Performance in a Mediatized Culture* (London: Routledge, 2008).

Brando, Marlon. *Songs My Mother Taught Me* (New York: Random House, 1994).

Brecht, Bertolt. *Brecht on Theatre* (London: Methuen, 1978).

Callow, Simon. *Being an Actor* (London: Vintage, 2004).

Chaikin, Joseph. *The Presence of the Actor* (New York: Theatre Communications Group, 1991).

Chekhov, Michael. *To the Actor: On the Technique of Acting* (London: Routledge, 2006).

Dench, Judi. *Scenes from my Life* (London: Weidenfeld & Nicholson, 2006).

Forsyth, Alison and Megson, Chris, eds. *Get Real: Documentary Theatre Past and Present* (Basingstoke: Palgrave Macmillan, 2009).

Frayn, Michael. *Stage Directions: Writing on Theatre, 1970–2008* (London: Faber, 2008).

Goodall, Jane. *Stage Presence* (Abingdon: Routledge, 2008).

Hodge, Alison. *Twentieth-Century Actor Training* (London: Routledge, 2000).

Leabhart, Thomas. *Etienne Decroux* (London: Routledge, 2007).

Lee-Wright, Peter. *The Documentary Handbook* (New York: Routledge, 2009).

Lovell, Alan and Kramer, Peter. *Screen-Acting* (London: Routledge, 1999).

Luckhurst, Mary and Moody, Jane, eds. *Theatre and Celebrity in Britain, 1660–2000* (New York: Palgrave Macmillan, 2005).

Luckhurst, Mary and Veltman, Chloe, eds. *On Acting: Interviews with Actors* (London : Faber & Faber, 2001).

Krasner, David and Saltz, David, eds. *Staging Philosophy: Intersections of Theater, Performance, and Philosophy* (Ann Arbor: University of Michigan Press, 2006).

Milling, Jane and Banham, Martin, eds. *Extraordinary Actors: Essays on Popular Performers* (Exeter: Exeter University Press, 2004).

Murray, Simon and Keefe, John. *Physical Theatres: A Critical Introduction* (London: Routledge, 2007), 1.

Paget, Derek. *True Stories? Documentary Drama on Radio, Screen and Stage* (Manchester and New York: Manchester University Press, 1990).

Paget, Derek. *No Other Way to Tell it: Dramadoc/Docudrama on Television* (Manchester: Manchester University Press, 1998).

Paget, Derek. 'Acting with Facts: Actors Performing the Real in British Theatre and Television since 1990. A Preliminary Report on a New Research Project', *Studies in Documentary Film*, Vol. 1. No.2, 2007.

Power, Cormac. *Presence in Play: A Critique of Theories of Presence in the Theatre* (Amsterdam: Rodopi, 2008).

Reinelt, Janelle G. and Roach, Joseph R. *Critical Theory and Performance* (Ann Arbor: University of Michigan, 2007).

Roach, Joseph. *The Player's Passion: Studies in the Science of Acting* (Newark: University of Delaware, 1985).

Roach, Joseph. *It* (Ann Arbor: University of Michigan, 2007).

Rojek, Chris. *Celebrity* (London: Reaktion Books, 2001).

Rosenthal, Alan. *Why Docudrama?: Fact-fiction on Film and TV* (Carbondale: Southern Illinois University Press, 1999).

Schall, Ekkehard. *The Craft of Theatre: Seminars and Discussions on Brechtian Theatre* (London: Methuen, 2008).

Sher, Antony. *The Year of the King* (London: Chatto & Windus, 1985).

Sher, Antony. *Beside Myself: An Actor's Life* (London: Nick Hern, 2009).

Stanislavski, Constantin. *An Actor Prepares*, trans. Elizabeth Reynolds Hapgood (London: Geoffrey Bles, 1958).

Stanislavski, Constantin. *Creating a Role*, trans. Elizabeth Reynolds Hapgood (London: Geoffrey Bles, 1961).

Stanislavski, Constantin. *Building a Character*, trans. Elizabeth Reynolds Hapgood (London: Methuen, 1968).

Thomson, Peter. *On Actors and Acting* (Exeter: University of Exeter, 2000).

West, Timothy. *A Moment Towards the End of the Play* (London: Nick Hern, 2001).